KEVIN WALLACE

AFTER THIS

CHARIS

AFTER THIS by Kevin Wallace
Published by Charisma House, an imprint of Charisma Media
600 Rinehart Road, Lake Mary, Florida 32746

Cover design contributor: Zeke Tucker

Visit the author's website at kevinwallace.live.

Cataloging-in-Publication Data is on file with the Library of Congress.
International Standard Book Number: 978-1-63641-076-0
E-book ISBN: 978-1-63641-077-7

21 22 23 24 25 — 98765432
Printed in the United States of America

Scripture quotations marked NRSV are from the New Revised Standard Version of the Bible. Copyright © 1989 by the Division of Christian Education of the National Council of the Churches of Christ in the USA. Used by permission.

Scripture quotations marked TPT are from The Passion Translation®. Copyright © 2017, 2018 by Passion & Fire Ministries, Inc. Used by permission. All rights reserved. ThePassionTranslation.com.

Cover design contributor: Zeke Tucker

Visit the author's website at kevinwallace.live.

Cataloging-in-Publication Data is on file with the Library of Congress.
International Standard Book Number: 978-1-63641-076-0
E-book ISBN: 978-1-63641-077-7

While the author has made every effort to provide accurate internet addresses at the time of publication, neither the publisher nor the author assumes any responsibility for errors or for changes that occur after publication. Further, the publisher does not have any control over and does not assume any responsibility for author or third-party websites or their content.

21 22 23 24 25 — 9 8 7 6 5 4 3 2 1
Printed in the United States of America

Contents

Foreword

WOULDN'T IT BE great if there were a vaccine for trouble? How wonderful would it be if there were a shot or pill we could take that would cause us to become immune to attack, problems, and hard, heart-breaking seasons? But sadly, that's just not the case. One thing I've learned in life is the reality of this. No one gets a pass from it, and for sure we all have to contend with trouble. No one is immune, and absolutely no one is insulated, not even Christ followers.

We all have had times in our lives when situations, issues, incidents, and accidents hit us with such intensity that we wondered how we would survive. The fallout was so great and the devastation so complete that we found ourselves asking, "Is this it? Or can there be an *after this*?" After this failure, after this financial crash, after this divorce, after this affair, after this abuse, after this devastation with my children, after this loss, will there ever be an *after this*?

An important thing to understand about the Lord is that He is in control, not just sometimes but all the time. Not one thing ever has taken or ever will take Him by surprise, and nothing will knock Him off His throne. In good times, bad times, high times, low times, bitter times, sweet times, and everything in between, God remains God, and He is in charge. Nothing shocks or unnerves Him, and nothing happens by accident. We all go through things we despise, but every believer must know, God would not have allowed it if He weren't going to use it.

As I look back across the years of my own life, I see the importance of hard times and difficult situations. I know from my experience that if God had not led me through those seasons, and even used those seasons, I never would have moved, changed, or stayed on course toward becoming the man He has called me to be. Something very important to remember is this: the struggles of our past and even today often prepare us for victories in our future.

The truth is, we don't grow in the good times; we grow in the tough times, the dark times, and the times that cause us to trust God with all our hearts. Even the times when I failed or just plain blew it, I look back on and rejoice. Why? Because God used it *all* to move me forward in His plan for my life.

It makes Paul's writings to the early church in Rome ring all the more true—"We know that all things work together for good to those who love God" (Rom. 8:28). Paul didn't say we hope, or we think, or even we are convinced that just maybe. On the contrary, Paul said emphatically, "*We know*".

There is blessed assurance when we know that all things are working together for our good. In the original Greek text of the New Testament, the phrase *works together* implies that something is made to cooperate. God was saying through Paul and to Paul, "I'm so big, so omniscient, and so omnipotent that I will make everything in your life cooperate with My divine plan and recipe for ultimate good as it relates to you." *All things* means simply that: *all things*! Our failures, frictions, and fractions all have to cooperate with God's plan for our lives.

That's why I love the message of this book—I've even preached it myself. The background of Revelation 4 is a powerful one as it relates to an *after this* moment. Imagine this scenario: The year is about AD 95. The ruling emperor is Titus Flavius Domitian. This godless emperor had demanded to be worshipped as lord and king. This old apostle of Christ, John the Beloved, who wrote the Book of Revelation, refused, and for that he was exiled to an island prison. The Bible says he was "on the island that is called Patmos" (Rev. 1:9).

The word *patmos* can be defined as the place of my killing or the dying place.[1] In the mind of Titus Flavius and everyone else's, this island called Patmos was John's dying place. This barren, dry rock was ten miles long and six miles wide. Patmos was a miserable place. Death, dying, torture, and torment were all around John. It would be hard for us to comprehend what this old apostle was enduring. It was rough, but it was not the end. It was a season; it was not a sentence.

Read what John declared in Revelation 4:1: "After this I looked, and there before me was a door standing open in heaven. And the voice I had first heard speaking to me like a trumpet said, 'Come up here, and I will show you what must take place after this'" (NIV). Perhaps you've had some trying and intense times lately. John can relate, but consider what he wrote. After this, John said, there was an open door. Something about all he had been through produced an open door in his life.

And not only that. John declared, "After this...the voice I had first heard speaking to me like a trumpet said, '*Come up here*'" (Rev. 4:1, NIV, emphasis added). After this, John moved up higher. After this time on Patmos, John wrote 1, 2, and 3 John. He was greatly used by God, and many Bible historians say he became the leader and bishop of the great New Testament church in Ephesus. But it all took place *after this*!

Society and religion want to judge you based on where you've been and where you are now, but don't you dare let them. There is an *after this* in your life. You don't have to live trapped in Patmos. God wants to open doors for you—doors of joy, healing, breakthrough, peace, power, direction, prosperity, and blessing! You don't have to stay where you are. After the struggle, the trouble, the pain, the problem, the pandemic, and the predicament, you can rise, in Jesus' name.

Be encouraged. This is not the final act or the end for your life, for your destiny is greater than your dilemma and your purpose is greater than your pain. Read the next pages and allow your heart to be infused with faith, victory, and joy! It's not over. There are some things that *must* take place *after this.*

—Jim Raley

Lead Pastor, Calvary Christian Center

Acknowledgments

WRITING A BOOK is a big deal. This work would not have been possible without the love and understanding of my amazing family and some incredible kingdom connections who assisted me in its completion.

To my wife, Deven—where would I be without you? Your wisdom and prayers are the difference makers in our family. Thanks for being such a great mom and caretaker of our home during this project and in every season of our lives. You have been a rock, and I am grateful to God for your love, patience, and wisdom. I love you!

To my kids, Jeremiah, Isaiah, Zion, Judah, and Genesis—thank you for your sweet and understanding hearts. You shared your dad time with everyone who will read this book and be blessed by it. I have asked God to pour out His blessing on each of your lives. I am grateful God gave me the most amazing children in the world. I'm so proud of you all!

To Richie Hughes—thanks for inspiring me to write this book and knowing what to do with the finished product. I will never forget it!

To Patrick Conley—thank you for your invaluable insight, your literary prowess, and your heart for the kingdom of God. I couldn't have done this without you.

To Zeke Tucker—thank you for your stellar graphic work on the book cover.

To the Redemption to the Nations Church leadership team—thank you for the transcribing, the surveys, the discussions, and the input that helped me complete this assignment. I love you all to life!

To the Redemption to the Nations Church family—it has been the honor of my life to lead such a beautiful tribe of Jesus people. You are my kingdom family. Thank you for being an incubator that watched the development of a young preacher kid. For almost twenty years we have grown together and witnessed the most incredible miracles and blessings. I love you all dearly. Thanks for being the seedbed of this book and the others that will follow.

Introduction

I HAVE NEVER LIVED outside of Tennessee. In fact, for most of my life I have resided within an hour's drive of Chattanooga. I was raised there, graduated high school there, went to college there, met my wife and got married there, and am raising my kids in Tennessee. Although I have traveled thousands of miles, there is no place like the Volunteer State for me. At the end of every trip, whether my plane is landing in Chattanooga or I am making the drive on Interstate 75, I am always glad when the familiar skyline and mountain ridges tell me I am home.

We live in Ooltewah, a quaint, almost sleepy bedroom community of Chattanooga that is tucked into the southern tip of the Appalachian mountain range. The friendliness of its people and a backdrop of beautiful scenery make our town a great place to live. One of the things we most appreciate about our region is that we get to enjoy the full gamut of seasons and the unique beauty they each bring. Of course, the seasons also have their distinctive difficulties. We get to slide on the ice and snow in the winter, spend spring fighting pollen (which seems to accumulate as high as the winter's snow), bake on the near-triple-digit summer days, and rake leaves every fall. As predictable as sunrise and sunset, the cycle of seasons never ends.

Seasons change but not quickly. Certainly on some fall mornings, a chill can seem to have arrived abruptly. On late-winter afternoons, the sun can seem to have a warmth that is more May than March. Those weather previews aside, the seasonal changes do not arrive suddenly, at least not typically. Slow and almost undetected, completely lacking in drama, we shift from season to season one degree and a few minutes of daylight at a time. Yet as slow as their passing may be, the seasons do pass.

This consistency of change brings a reality that can be either pleasant or unfortunate. If you love the current season, the bad news is that it will not last forever. If you hate the season you are in, the good news is that it will not last forever. Whether you are saying goodbye to the beautiful summer days that you adore or good riddance to the frigid temperatures and snowy hazards of winter that you despise, in due time the season will change.

The beauty of Tennessee's seasonal shifts is not so different from anywhere else on the map. No matter where you live, and in ways that have nothing to do with climate, life has a way of changing seasons as well. Sometimes the change can feel devastating, a hard hit that feels totally unfair. At other times, the change inaugurates new life, bringing us a fresh dose of joy and hope. On some occasions we find ourselves experiencing great success, moments in which we feel as if we are living in showers of blessing. But we also have seasons of tragic loss, abject failure, unimaginable suffering, and debilitating frustration.

The seasons of life, spiritual and emotional, have one thing that is unlike the natural seasons. In the world of temperatures and precipitation, the seasons are rather predictable, designed by God to follow certain patterns. This allows us to know with some consistency how long these seasons will be and when they will end. But with the seasons of our lives, we do not have this luxury. Some of our seasons are long and drawn out, while others are short and pronounced.

Most of you know what it is like to be in a place from which you wish you could escape. Maybe you are there now. If so, I wrote this book for you, one who feels stuck in a difficult season. Maybe it is a ministry place. Maybe it is relational. Or it could be financial, spiritual, or any number of things. Whatever the season you find yourself in, God has something in store for you. I call it "after this."

I am confident in telling you that you have not yet experienced the greatest season of your life. I know it is a bold statement, but I believe it—and not as some pie-in-the-sky, wishful thought. This belief is firmly rooted in the truth of God's Word and the identity of God Himself. Your best season is ahead.

Perhaps I should offer a qualifier to that statement. I did not say it will be the easiest, most relaxing, or calmest season you have ever encountered. Nonetheless, I have no doubt that the God of unfolding, unending glory has yet to reveal the fullness of His goodness in your life.

Some may imagine that I am speaking about a hollow, materialistic kind of season, one so shallow that you find yourself feeling as if you're sitting in a kiddie pool with lots of toys, all the while wishing for deeper waters. That is not what I have in mind. Stepping into a greater season is less about having more things and more about thriving because you are possessing a wholeness and strength that come only from God.

A moment is coming in which your life will come into greater alignment, your steps will become more divinely ordered, and your Christ-centered ambitions and efforts will become increasingly favored.

As a recreational golfer, I spend most of my time trying to find the sweet spot on the golf club. When I hit the ball with the sweet spot, it goes further, is more accurately placed, and sounds better than when I hit it on the toe or heel of the club. The odd thing is, I usually hit the sweet spot when I swing smoother, not harder. Having a controlled pace is more important than trying to kill the ball.

The secret to hitting with the sweet spot is not swinging harder; it is continuing to swing. No matter how many times you hit the ball into the water on the first hole, you just pick the ball up, move to the second hole, and swing again, searching for that sweet spot. Nothing keeps me coming back for the next round of golf like hitting the ball with the sweet spot.

We are about to find the sweet spot on our journey with Jesus. It does not matter how many times you missed it.

Forget the previous season. Let go of the feeling it gave you. Get back in the game and swing again. Whatever you do, do not stop. This place you are in is not permanent. There is an *after this*.

My job is not simply to persuade you to believe that. I sense an assignment to remind you that you may have forgotten that God is good. Remember what Paul said in Galatians 6:9: "And let us not grow weary while doing good, for in due season we shall reap if we do not lose heart." Let me encourage you to prepare yourself for the thing God has been working on, both in you and for you.

I am not sure what your world has felt like recently, but I have noticed a collective assault against our hope. I have witnessed an unleashing of assassins of our future who have an agenda to drain our dreams and destroy the expectations we have for divinely blessed tomorrows.

Whether it has been the barrage of images, stats, and reports regarding the carnage and collateral damage associated with the COVID-19 pandemic or the unrest and division that has permeated virtually every conversation in our society, the truth is we are living in challenging times. Hardly a day goes by during which we do not see something that makes our hearts sink or causes our minds to be invaded with worry.

In addition to the challenges that our world is going through, I have noticed an increase in the spiritual conflict being experienced by children of God. While some would be quick to reject such a notion or pretend that we are exempt from warfare on this spiritual journey, a transparent and honest assessment of our lives reveals that those who love Christ and walk by faith at times find themselves being resisted and assailed by the enemy.

What is the response of the believer in such moments? The key to operating in victory and thriving in this climate is to guard our vision, protect the expectation we have for a better future, and keep the faith. Paul alludes to this reality in Ephesians 6 when he encourages us to put on the whole armor of God. He does not tell us to put on the armor so we will be culturally hip and socially relevant. He says to arm ourselves so that we will be able to stand. Too many people have lost their ability to stand. We quit too early. We give up too soon.

When I think about those who have the ability to stand, to keep on believing, I am reminded of a sweet saint who was part of our church family for decades. Betty Johnson was a church mother who worked for the Lord nearly all her life. She often encouraged her pastor and anyone else who preached the gospel from our pulpit with expressions of affirmation as they preached the Word. She confirmed the message with a frequent "Amen!" and other key spiritual phrases to encourage the minister and the church during the delivery of the message.

I will never forget my favorite phrase that she ever said. One Sunday, I was preaching about the "more of God." As I was laying the foundation for all that God had in store for His people, I said, "Many people cannot comprehend the greatness of what God is getting ready to do in their lives. Their minds cannot receive it." Without hesitation Mother Betty Johnson stood up and said, "Lord, bless their feeble minds!"

That is my prayer for you. No matter the journey, the dead ends, the bad reports, the spiritual conflicts, or the closed doors you encounter, I pray that your mind would be so blessed that you stand, you stick with it, and you see the next season of blessing and greatness that God has for you.

There is an *after this* coming no matter what you have endured or are currently fighting through. Satan may have planted the thought in you that you will never recover. In this book I intend to uproot that lie and plant seeds of hope as I introduce you to revelation that produces greater expectation for your future.

Many people are familiar with the story of Joseph. His life seemed like a roller coaster at times and offers us a clear picture of the ups and downs in the life of a person who walked in the goodness of God. His journey began with unexplainable favor from his father and a dream from God. As Joseph's story unfolds, we discover that pain and disloyalty are part of the journey that led him to fulfilled dreams.

BUT *AFTER*

After Joseph had been through betrayal, alienation, and the shame of being sold into slavery by his brothers, he was eventually promoted to a place of honor and prestige as the viceroy of Egypt. When the world was thrown into a famine, everyone was forced to go to Egypt to find food for their survival. This situation resulted in the reuniting of Joseph with his brothers. As they came into his presence to buy food from him, Genesis 42:8 says, "Joseph recognized his brothers, but they did not recognize him."

Perhaps they thought he would look defeated and run-down at this point in his journey. After all, he had spent time in a pit, a prison, and Potiphar's house. But he did not look like the pit he was left in, the inmate that he was in prison, or the scoundrel he was accused of being with Potiphar's wife.

They did not recognize him as the Pharaoh's right-hand man because that isn't how they remembered him. They remembered leaving him alone and in slavery and could not recognize him in a place of prominence and favor. In short, he didn't look like what he had been through. You may feel as if the pit and the prison left an indelible mark on your life, but the grace of God is in operation, and you will not look like all you have been through.

This book is a product of the challenges, tests, and adversarial environments I have walked through on my journey. Please make no mistake about it, the Lord has been good to me. I have experienced the kindness and blessing of God in ways that have blown my mind. But often we suspect those who have experienced a modicum of the favor of God to be people who have been exempt from real challenges and pain. That is not the case.

We do not remember Peter for denying Jesus three times. We remember him for his day of Pentecost sermon, the souls he won, and the epistles he wrote for our spiritual development. All those pieces of his legacy happened *after* his greatest failure.

We do not remember Lazarus for dying, stinking, and being entombed in graveclothes. We remember him for being a friend of Jesus who was in a tomb in John chapter

11, then, after being raised from the dead, was sitting at the table with Jesus by the next chapter. We do not remember Rahab and her harlotries. We do remember a woman who cooperated with the spies of Israel, hid them from their enemy, and secured her place in the hall of faith (Heb. 11:31). Mary Magdalene could have been known by her promiscuity and the demons that were cast out of her. Instead, she is enshrined in church history as a follower of Jesus who was the first witness of the empty tomb (John 20:1–2).

The point is, if you are breathing, God is still writing the story of your life. See the Mary glory in your future. If you are not dead, Jesus is not done. You will see it *after this*.

CHAPTER 1

Scattered

SCATTERED. WHY BEGIN a book with such a disturbing thought?

At first glance, you may see no need to read a chapter with this name. After all, you might have everything together right now. You might be so blessed that even when the lives of people around you have been flung into disorder, your world is stable and constant. If so, please stay with me. Resist the temptation to bail out on this part of the journey by skipping ahead. If you are not walking through a difficult season now, it will arrive soon enough. Then you will need the truth you will find here.

Have you been told that following Jesus exempts you from seasons of persecution and pain? The reality is, no matter how positive our confessions are and how excited we are when we say them, even the godliest among us have experienced tremendous trials and have faced the threats of hell on our journeys. Being scattered, experiencing havoc, and facing adversities are part of life on earth. But when you do face these, the clarity you will find here will be a steadfast anchor amid the chaos.

Yes, this is a chapter about turbulence. But triumph is coming.

THE MODEL CHURCH

The New Testament Book of Acts tells the history of the beginning of the church. Luke, the physician who wrote it, details the church's birth and foundational years with great care and precision. His careful recording notwithstanding, the Book of Acts is far from being a mere catalog of historical events in the lives of those early believers. Acts is the articulation of the kingdom paradigm. Its pages reveal what the daily lives of congregations and the Christians within them should look like.

Famous Christian author and scholar C. S. Lewis said, "A man does not call a line crooked unless he has some idea of a straight line."[1] In other words, in order to evaluate what is, we must know what ought to be. When we want to know what the Christian community ought to be like in our generation, we look to the Book of Acts.

To explore this model church, we must look past its practices that applied solely to that time and place, such as meeting exclusively in houses or synagogues. I do not advocate launching archaeological expeditions to determine whether the early church used pews or chairs, and I am not going to instruct our worship leaders to limit the Sunday song set to first-century hymns. Methods and strategies have certainly changed. That is to be expected. Nonetheless, Acts is still the blueprint for God's people.

Imagine a church that modeled itself after the church in Acts. Picture what it would look like if every church followed the blueprint of operating in signs, miracles, and wonders. What if our prayer meeting was the most-attended meeting of the week? What if our gatherings were known for launching evangelists and missionaries? What if worship experiences lasted all night? What if the next time we went to the church, our leaders told everyone to wait and pray until God's power and presence were manifested in a tangible way?

That is what church was like in the Book of Acts. How amazing it must have been to have experienced the crescendo of kingdom movement as revival broke out! The outpouring of the Holy Spirit caused the church to grow from 120 gathered in the Upper Room into a movement that swept throughout the region. The preachers in the early church were not caught up in rhetorical competitions. Their goal was not to impress the crowds with their dynamic delivery. Their sermon content was simple and straightforward: Jesus Christ!

On the day of Pentecost, after those in the Upper Room were baptized in the Holy Spirit, Peter preached to the gathering onlookers. I would sum up his message in Acts 2:14–36 this way: "You crucified Him. You buried Him. But God raised Him from the dead! He is alive! We have seen Him! Now, repent and be saved!"

The message was as powerful as it was simple. Every time it was preached, a harvest of souls came into the kingdom of God. Thousands who came to faith spread the gospel to their friends and families. The Jewish temple was transformed from a space focused on rigid, religious protocol into the epicenter of gospel power. The miraculous story of a lame man being healed in the name of Jesus swept throughout Jerusalem. Apostles were preaching on the streets, new converts were sharing their faith in the marketplace, and the truth of Jesus fulfilling the Scriptures was even being taught on the steps of the temple itself.

The first portion of Acts reveals a church exploding in growth as "the Lord added to the church daily those who were being saved" (Acts 2:47). The church was growing so quickly that the apostles were on the verge of being overwhelmed by the needs of this new congregation. Church leaders quickly recognized that if they were going to have a healthy church community, structure was essential. They had more growth, people, and ministry opportunities than they knew what to do with. What a wonderful problem!

Don't you love those times of abundance in life? Have you ever been in a season in which everything you touched found favor? When we as ministry leaders find ourselves there, we cling to those moments with all our strength. It is in those seasons that we feel close to God. We feel anointed and fulfilled. The sense that our labors are consequential energizes us to do even more. These are the highlight-reel moments of our lives.

That is exactly where the early church members found themselves in the Book of Acts. They were accused of turning the world upside down (Acts 17:6). This was no inconsequential group of nobodies and misfits who were quietly gathering to discuss their marginalized belief system. No; these people were getting things done! With no printing press, no satellites, no blue check marks, and not even a savvy marketing strategy, these ambassadors of heaven were pioneering an invasion by the kingdom of God through the power of the Holy Spirit.

HARDSHIP AND ADVERSITIES

You might imagine that a church with such noble priorities and such a profound impact would have some sort of immunity to adversity and attack. Our train of thought goes something like this: "Because I belong to God and God is good, everything in my life will move forward without resistance or opposition."

If your inner dialogue sounds like that, you are not alone. This fallacious expectation has emerged because of lopsided teaching in the body of Christ. One of the church's greatest tragedies is that much of Western theology about adversity is contrary to kingdom reality. Somehow, out of self-serving attitudes or ignorance or both, we have created a gospel that promotes comfort and prioritizes convenience for the individual rather than a wholistic understanding of how God works in our lives. I often see teachers and preachers migrate to their favorite texts as proof of the perpetual bliss that awaits the child of God in this life. And like many other things in the Western world, it sells.

I would love to tell you that Christianity is the spiritual equivalent of Disney's Magic Kingdom, "the most magical place on earth." I love people, and that means I hate to see them hurt or disappointed. I wish I could tell you that conversion meant instant paradise in your daily life. But I cannot because I have read the Book of Acts.

Acts is a great counterbalance to unhealthy, theological imbalance. The writer never attempts to sanitize the pain of these devoted Christians, nor is there any attempt to water down the accounts of persecution they experienced. Affliction is never presented as some strange occurrence. On the contrary, terrible suffering seemed to be the norm for believers in Acts. The hardships experienced by the early church reveal an uncomfortable truth: godly, favored, and anointed people still encounter challenges and opposition.

In our world of positive affirmations and optimistic thinking, the content of this first chapter may seem like an unnecessary negative confession that we are not inclined to consider, much less embrace. But I want to say this clearly: if you have experienced pain and frustration, if you have ever felt disappointment and discouragement, please stop telling yourself that means you are not blessed and highly favored by God. We need to cultivate a more robust theology regarding suffering and pain. We should not become obsessed with anguish. I certainly do not propose that we spend our days wallowing in despair. However, we must stop getting so offended and shocked when setbacks and hardships occur.

Discipleship is not an adventure in self-fulfillment and self-aggrandizement. True faith is not contingent on the size and scope of the "Christian benefits package" we receive when we enter the kingdom. True Book of Acts faith is walking the path of commitment when we can barely see through the tears. It is lifting our voices in praise when we feel a lump of disappointment in our throats. It is doing the right thing even when our skin is stinging from the falling cinders of our burned-up plans. This faith is lifting our hands in surrender and worship when pain is gripping our hearts. It is trusting God when it feels as if everything else we had confidence in let us down. This Acts kind of faith is understanding that just because God did not keep us *from* the trial does not mean He cannot keep us *through* it.

Of course, it is one thing to talk about walking in faith when you are reading a book about it and quite another when you are blindsided by trouble. That is exactly what happened in Acts. The disciples were in the middle of making history for the glory of God. They were literally walking out the greatest story ever told. They saw mass salvations, incredible miracles, and the greatest outpouring of the Holy Spirit the world had ever seen. Then, seemingly out of nowhere, the story turned on its head.

In Acts chapters 6 and 7 we find the story of Stephen. He is one of seven believers chosen to serve the early church. He performed signs and wonders but was opposed by some Jews who argued with him. They brought him before the Sanhedrin on false charges of blasphemy. During a captivating defense, Stephen accused the Jewish leaders of resisting the Holy Spirit. He was dragged out of the city and stoned.

In the next few sentences a handful of riveting phrases reveal what happened next:

> At that time a great persecution arose against the church which was at Jerusalem; and they were all scattered throughout the regions of Judea and Samaria, except the apostles. And devout men carried Stephen to his burial, and made great lamentation over him. As for Saul, he made havoc of the church, entering every house, and dragging off men and women, committing them to prison.
>
> —ACTS 8:1–3

When reading Acts chapter 8, we must be careful not to write this off as an isolated attack reserved for the first-century Christians who pioneered the work of the kingdom in their generation. Nothing could be further from the truth. Their suffering was not unique to their city or even to their time. It was simply part of their Christian journey. In fact, we would have a hard time finding any time or place in Scripture, or even in the entirety of church history, in which true disciples did not experience some hardship.

Even our Lord Himself prepared us for this sobering reality when, in John 15:20, He said, "Remember the word that I said to you: 'A servant is not greater than his master.' If they persecuted Me, they will also persecute you."

We must never forget that as children of the light who advance the kingdom of God, we are living in an antagonistic world filled with opposition, hostility, and persecution. If you require affirmation from the world, you will find yourself living in frustration and isolation. In fact, Jesus told us we should expect to be hated by the world around us (John 15:18–19). You may think that being hated by the entire system around us does not sound like "American health, wealth, and happiness Christianity" at all! You would be right. If you are looking for a way to avoid discomfort in your life, Christianity is not the place to go.

DISTURBING WORDS

If the gospel you have heard preached has been the fiction of earthly bliss instead of the good news of heavenly hope, then reading this chapter may be disturbing to you. Becoming disturbed is the most common reaction for a Western Christian reading the Book of Acts. In fact, tucked into the chapters of Acts are a number of disturbing words.

Persecution

First, Luke describes the early Christians as facing seasons of *persecution*. The concept of persecution is that someone or something is chasing you to harm you. To paint the picture, Luke uses the Greek word *diōgmos*. Pardon the lecture, but the root of *diōgmos* is the word *diōkō*, which describes the act of pursuing an object of prey in war or while hunting.[2]

Persecution is not an arbitrary bad day. It is a full-throttle attack that has you running for your life, crashing through the underbrush of confusion, miles from the well-beaten path of your best-laid plans while the vicious hounds of hell bay the news that they are on your trail. Being persecuted means never feeling relaxed or enjoying the moment lest you be caught off guard. It is lying awake at night while everyone else in your house sleeps because your problems are singing a duet with your fears, caterwauling the ballad of your destruction. The believers in Acts were on the run like prey being hunted, chased, and pursued. They lived in constant fear of being stalked by something out to destroy them. Being harassed and hindered, fleeing like prey—that is the feeling of persecution.

In Psalms chapter 3 David is running from Absalom when he cries out, "LORD, how they have increased who trouble me! Many are they who rise up against me. Many are they who say of me, 'There is no help for him in God'" (vv. 1–2). Have you ever been there? Have you ever felt pursued or surrounded? That is Acts persecution.

Havoc

As if feeling that prey was not bad enough, Saul "made havoc of the church, entering every house, and dragging off men and women, committing them to prison" (Acts 8:3). Though Saul later had a transformative experience with Jesus and served the church as the apostle Paul, in this part of the story he was a zealous Pharisee, creating havoc by hunting down Christians.

First, what is *havoc*? Perhaps you are thinking, "I don't know what it is, but I want nothing to do with it!" I am right there with you. If persecution is the pursuit, havoc is what happens when the prey is finally caught. In fact, when Luke says Saul "made havoc" (Acts 8:3), he uses the Greek word *lymainō* to describe what Saul was doing. It is an intense word, used only here in the entire New Testament. In the Greek translations of the Old Testament, this word is used in reference to "wild beasts, such as lions, bears, and leopards tearing at raw flesh."[3]

Havoc is when the thing you feared happens. It is being caught in the flashing whirlwind of teeth and claws as lions tear you limb from limb and all chance of escape is gone. It is when the doctor says, "Cancer"; the mechanic says, "Bad transmission"; the boss says, "Fired"; and your spouse says, "Divorce"—all in the same month. When the very fabric of your life—the dependable people, places, and routines—are shredded by a marauding enemy, that is havoc.

Havoc is precisely how to describe the situation the saints found themselves in. Pardon the piling on, but this havoc was not an isolated event. In Acts 8:3 the verb translated as "make havoc" or "to ravage" is an imperfect verb. That means Saul was ravaging in an ongoing sense. Scholar James Boice described it this way: "He ravaged it and kept on ravaging it."[4] There seemed to be no end in sight. Every time they turned around, they found the enemy on their heels. You have heard the saying "Out of the frying pan and into the fire." In Acts the church was fleeing from a fire to a bigger fire, repeatedly.

Perhaps the most ominous observance about this season is that Saul made havoc in "every house" (Acts 8:3). The enemy literally invaded homes. This was not just an attack on the corporate body of believers. No; this onslaught involved ravaging individual households.

When we are trying to advance the kingdom, one of Satan's greatest strategies is to wreak havoc among those who are closest to us and who matter the most. Nothing can distract or hinder us like a spiritual home invasion. When someone's home has been broken into, he or she often describes the feeling as having been violated—suddenly feeling unsafe in the place that is supposed to be a refuge, a place of respite in the midst of a tumultuous world. Few things are more effective at invoking fear than destroying the feeling of being safe at home.

The enemy is aware of our dependence on home. Furthermore, having observed the modus operandi of God's operation in the courts of heaven, Satan knows that kingdom structure is predicated on home structure. If you do not believe me, you have to look no further than the attack on the family in the garden. Thus, the home is often the highest-value target on hell's hit list. If you have ever been through a real battle in your home, you know just how difficult it can be.

Some of you are in the middle of a home invasion right now. Someone reading this feels as if the enemy is harassing and chasing him or her. Your house may be caught in the crosshairs of demonic attack. The home that was your place of peace has become a war zone. The people closest to you are under attack, perhaps in their health and their mental well-being. Anxiety is at an all-time high, and the pressures of the day have made communication a minefield. Maybe your children are under spiritual onslaught. Maybe your marriage is under fire. Maybe things have come against your family that you never imagined you would face. If that is you, do not be surprised. Attacking your home is a common tactic of the enemy, particularly if you are a threat to Satan and his work. I am not saying it is easy. I would not wish "home havoc" on anyone. But there is help in the pages ahead.

We should take a moment and recognize how the enemy

works. First, the kingdom of darkness does not waste time on people who are not a threat. If you are experiencing any kind of persecution or havoc, stop right now and recognize it as an attack whose intent is to keep you from moving forward. The enemy is not wasting war on you. You would not be in this fight if you were not an existential threat to Satan and his destructive agenda. If the enemy is trying to terrorize your *present,* then he is terrified of your *potential*.

Second, you are not being attacked because you are *forgotten*. Instead, you are being attacked because you are *favored*. Favor attracts both blessings and enemies. In 2 Samuel 5:17 the Bible says, "When the Philistines heard that David had been anointed king over Israel, they went up in full force to search for him" (NIV). His inauguration into authority was an invitation for opposition. Can you imagine receiving an anointing from God and that blessing becoming the very summons sent to your enemies, announcing that the time for attacking you had come? That was David's experience.

Jesus also experienced this conflation of blessing and opposition. In Matthew 3:16–17 we read that as soon as Jesus was baptized and came up out of the water, heaven was opened and the Spirit of God descended on Him like a dove. "A voice from heaven said, 'This is my Son, whom I love; with him I am well pleased'" (NIV).

What a moment for Jesus! I cannot imagine a more victorious event. Heaven opens. The Holy Spirit descends. The Father breaks through the barrier of time and space to announce in the earthly realm that Jesus is indeed the Son who is beloved by the Father. Yet the next verse declares, "Then Jesus was led up into the wilderness by the Spirit to be tempted by the devil" (Matt. 4:1, MEV).

How could that possibly be the next verse? It does not even seem logical. Why all the affirmation and honor if the next moment is going to be the trial of a lifetime? But that is exactly the way God planned it, even though it may have seemed as if the monumental moment of affirmation served as an invitation for the wilderness temptation.

Scattered

So far we have witnessed the enemy's efforts to stifle any prospect of God's kingdom and His righteousness being advanced. We can picture the heartbreaking procession as Stephen's bruised and broken body is carried to a tomb. We can hear wailing women as their husbands are hauled off to face the authorities. We can see grandparents trying to hide their fear from their grandbabies as the news of Saul and his terrible mission spreads through the community. Yes, we can imagine saints running for their lives, looking for places to hide, begging for people to take them in, for someone to get them to a safe city. We have seen some dark things.

The final word that describes the unfolding season that we witness in Acts 8 is *scattered*. In fact, twice chapter 8 reports that the people of God were *scattered* (vv. 1, 4). First persecution, then havoc, and now the people of God are forced to flee from the comfort of their homes. Their lives are totally disrupted. Their plans are eviscerated, their dreams are jeopardized, and their futures look bleak.

They found themselves in unfamiliar environments, away from the security of home.

They had been scattered.

The early church enjoyed community among the believers in Jerusalem. Realistically, who would want to leave this church? All the apostles were there—the greatest preachers of the day. They had experienced vibrant growth in number and were riding a wave of tremendous momentum. Signs and wonders were abounding, pastoral care was taking place, and Christian fellowship was readily available. It was powerful. It was safe. Leave? No thank you; this church is awesome!

No matter how amazing the Jerusalem church was, the ministry of the gospel was never intended to be confined to one place. Perhaps the church at Jerusalem seems familiar to us because it did church in ways that match our modern ideology. How many came? How many stayed? How do we connect to new believers and keep them satisfied so they never even think about leaving? Sometimes, even unconsciously, the church can position itself in ways that cause it to miss the missional assignment Jesus called it to.

When the church is myopic and self-focused, the focal point can become a pursuit of creature comforts rather than gospel expansion. When the church is missing the target, God will work through whatever drastic measure necessary to realign His people with their God-given purpose. Although I would never suggest God sent the persecution the early church experienced, He certainly worked through it in ways that made the church more effective and more of a spiritual force to be reckoned with.

ADVANCE IN ADVERSITY

We may not recognize it, but in Acts chapter 8 we witness God sovereignly working behind the scenes to catapult His gospel to places and people who might never have been reached without the suffering that forced the scattering of the believers.

Let us remind ourselves that we are not involved in a myopic, me-centered movement that focuses on self-preservation. We are part of an advancing tribe of people who have been called to go into all the world and disciple nations (Matt. 28:19–20). God worked through the persecution to plant gospel seeds all over that region. Without the persecution, the first believers might well have remained a centralized church, stuck in Jerusalem with limited influence and capacity. That was not God's plan, so He allowed them to be scattered.

Two words are used for *scattering.* One describes the kind of scattering you do when you throw fireplace ashes out the back door. The other kind describes the intentional act of scattering seed.[5] The first is done with no thought of future purpose. The second is done with the harvest in mind. That is precisely the kind of scattering that Dr. Luke had in mind when he said the church was scattered. It was not that God sent persecution to destroy the church and cast it out like burned-up ashes. They were not *forgotten*; they were *favored*. God saw the potential of the church and refused to allow it to limit its effectiveness by staying stuck in a place of comfort.

Maybe this story sounds familiar to you. Perhaps things

were going well, so you settled into blessed and peaceful times. Then suddenly an unexpected storm arose on the sea of your life. Maybe your ministry was sailing along with success, and then a pandemic hit, leaving you with an empty building and an even emptier heart. Perhaps your house seemed so blessed. The smiles in the family pictures were genuine. Then your son or daughter grew distant, and one day the dreaded call came: overdose. Maybe your life was a dream, the envy of all your friends, and out of nowhere the enemy attacked and left you devastated by divorce or rocked by a spouse's infidelity. Was it bankruptcy? Was it a failed business launch? Was it a career failure? Was it the sudden revelation of a hidden betrayal? Whatever it was, yours is not an isolated story of sorrow. These faithful first-century Christians went through it too.

We are called and created to advance in adversity. Realizing this will help you make sense out of the messy seasons of life. This should especially resonate for those of you who have asked, "Why is this happening?" That was the question I found myself mulling over as I dove deeper into this text: "Why are these New Testament believers experiencing this season of attack?"

If you have ever watched football, you have occasionally missed seeing all the action during a consequential play. The broadcast team helps you out by showing a zoomed-out replay showing the entire field of action. Only then can you grasp the series of movements that led to the triumphant moment. In the same way, when reading the Bible, we often find ourselves confused until we "zoom out" to get a view of the story in the context of the entire redemptive narrative of Scripture.

Perhaps right now God is allowing you to be stretched and challenged but not so that you will throw in the towel. You are mightier than you know. This season is proof of that. Instead, He is working to position you for greater kingdom effectiveness and maximum spiritual impact. Your present circumstances have not been in line with your potential. So you are being scattered.

In His sovereign love, God used the evil persecution of Saul and those who hated the church to advance the kingdom. The havoc and hell that the early church encountered positioned it for an explosion of growth. Without the scattering, the gospel might have died out in a few generations. They did not understand what God was doing. But through their pain, God was redeeming the world.

Hear me! *What you survive will serve you*. What does not kill you will wish it never messed with you. You have been scattered, but not like meaningless ashes that announce God is through with you. Quite the opposite. As for Jesus, for David, and for the early church, this season is not the end of you. It is the beginning of your most effective moments. The pain, the persecution, and every weapon that the enemy has used against you has pushed you out of the place where you wanted to be. If you are honest, you admit that you would have stayed in your comfort zone. But God sees much more in you than you see in yourself. That is why you are being scattered.

Some of God's greatest preparation is done while we are unaware. But very soon you will see the handiwork of

God in the seasons you were sure you would never successfully escape. In fact, Abba is going to use your season of pain to position you for the greatest sowing and reaping season of your life. If He allowed the enemy to chase you out of your Jerusalem, then make the enemy pay by sowing gospel seeds and fulfilling gospel purposes everywhere you go.

When you understand this, the times of turbulence make sense. Grasp this, and you will understand what our sovereign Abba has been doing during the seasons of threat and opposition. You have been scattered, but now get ready to grow.

First, looking deeper in your *this* seasons can position you to be prepared and used by God.

CHAPTER 2

What Is *This*?

THE STORY OF the first-century church members running for their lives may not have been an experience you can relate to in your life. I get it. Many of us are blessed to live in a free country. We cannot imagine persecution with the arrests, home invasions, and public executions that Saul and his entourage perpetrated while trying to extinguish the gospel fire. Yet the reality remains that all of us have a *this* chapter in our lives.

This is a unique word, general yet specific, comprehensive yet precise. *This* can represent a myriad of issues and circumstances. But for this context, we will narrow the focus to those make-or-break situations that we all face.

I have indeed experienced the favor of God in remarkable ways. But just like you, I have walked through a number of seasons I could refer to as *this* seasons. During one *this* season, my wife was sick, my one-year-old son had kidney stones, and my newborn had spinal meningitis—all at the same time. I have endured *this* seasons of betrayal. I have trekked through *this* times of loneliness and fear. I am not sharing this to gain pity or praise but so you will understand that I too have been through some *this*.

MY *THIS* SEASON

Walking through those grueling times might have left me thinking that I had already encountered the biggest enemies and fought the biggest battles, that I was well past any *this* seasons. But one of the most difficult periods of *this* I have ever passed through occurred when I battled COVID-19.

Though some view COVID-19 as a political fabrication or overreach, I can unequivocally say I have never been that sick in my life. It was not just a physical struggle; it was a spiritual battle with the enemy as well. Never have I been more certain that I was caught up in an otherworldly conflict. Even as my body fought off the dreaded virus, my soul faced a hellish barrage. While the infection sought to starve my lungs of oxygen, the enemy tried to choke the life from my spirit. It was a war.

On a Monday afternoon I began to feel a bit strange. I thought I was coming down with something mild or that I just needed some rest. Then I noticed that I could not taste anything.

"OK," I thought. "That's only one of the symptoms. Let me see if I can smell anything."

I looked around for things I knew had aromas. A few sniffs revealed that my sense of smell was also gone. Knowing these symptoms were sure signs of the virus, I immediately called my wife, Deven, and encouraged her and the kids to pack up and get away for a few days. I did not want my family to become sick too.

The next call was to my doctor, who is a man of God. He prayed with me, declared life over me, and prescribed both prescription and nonprescription medicine to equip my body for fighting off the sickness and to provide some relief from the more difficult symptoms that were likely to come. At this point, I was ready. I am a young man (even if my kids may not think so), and I am in good health. I had been prayed over, and I had my prescriptions. A week or so of quarantine for the sake of others, and COVID would be behind me—or so I thought. Little did I know what was heading my way.

To be honest, the first few days were uneventful. I had no sense of taste or smell, but other than being a little fatigued, I felt fairly normal. The worst part was reconciling with being locked away from everyone for nearly two weeks.

"This COVID thing is going to end up being no big deal for me," I thought. Oh, boy.

Have you ever watched cartoons and seen one of the characters run off a cliff, pump his legs in midair, and then look down and start to plummet? That is what my body did on day four when my biological systems looked down, realized that they had been infected, and commenced a rapid descent into misery. My eyes burned from within as my fever soared to 104.3 degrees. Deep throbbing aches settled in my muscles. My appetite was completely gone, and I even lost interest in drinking, which is a massive no-no. Good hydration is critical while your body fends off a virus. I was trying to fight it, but COVID was gaining the upper hand.

By day five, friends, colleagues, and kingdom family from all over the world heard I was sick. Calls began pouring in from everywhere with prayers and home remedies. This overwhelming display of concern from my kingdom family was encouraging. I was moved by the kindness shown to me, but I was growing weaker.

The sixth day was a Sunday. That morning, my oxygen levels dropped every time I got up to walk around. In what may not have been my best moment of decision making, I drove myself to the hospital. On the way, I prayed and believed, but mostly I just tried to breathe.

I am a pastor who started a church with thirty-four people, so I have not always had support staff and pastoral care teams to help care for the congregation. I know what it is to visit people in a hospital with sterile halls full of sickness and sometimes death. The parking, the check-in desk, even the layout and the lingo are all things with which I was acutely familiar. What was unfamiliar was the feeling that, this time, I was the one who was dying.

It was a Sunday I will never forget. I sat in an isolated room in the hospital, just four blocks away from my favorite place to be on Sunday—my church. COVID protocols meant that no one could accompany me. The necessary extra levels of protective equipment, masks, and face shields worn by those attending me separated me from their humanity. On a day when I am normally surrounded by hundreds of my favorite people on earth, I sat alone, struggling to breathe.

They wheeled me to a COVID room. Glancing at my watch, I saw that it was 10:44 a.m. I could imagine what my Redemption to the Nations church family was doing four blocks away. The worship team would be taking us to the throne, and the Holy Spirit would be shifting lives and changing destinies. I would be standing in the altar area with my bride, surrounded by people who were caught up in the heavenly experience of corporate worship. As the minutes ticked by, I went over every detail of what was happening in the house of worship I had been called to lead. Those thoughts were as painful as they were precious. That was my place of togetherness, yet here I sat, apart.

"Mr. Wallace, you have COVID," the doctor said, confirming what I already knew.

The doctor went on to explain the results of my lung X-ray and CT scan. When the novel coronavirus that causes COVID-19 first surfaced in China, there was no test for it. The doctors diagnosed the disease because this new strain of respiratory infection presented with symptoms that included opaque, glassy patches in lung scans.[1] Now, even though tests had been developed, scans were used to help diagnose the severity of the case.

When the doctor showed me the images of my chest, I noticed that my lungs looked as if they had neatly cut stripes running across them, like the stripes on a football field. He explained that the bad news was that my lungs revealed the glassy, opaque substance that had made my breathing difficult. The good news was that my lungs were not full. I was just grateful to have some good news to hold on to.

Since I had struggled so badly to breathe, I thought they would admit me. But every time they checked my oxygen, the saturation numbers were between 94 and 97. They had been much lower when I checked them at home in the days before that, but while I was there, they never dropped into what was considered the danger zone. I recognized later that the goodness of God kept me out of the hospital. As much as I wanted oxygen to breath, the last thing I needed was a respirator. The doctor sent me home with some more medication. Little did I realize, the battle had just begun.

THE BATTLE OF FAITH

If the physical battle were not enough, I now found myself at war in my mind and spirit. I tried to sleep, but my breathing had worsened to the point of being extremely labored. I went over seventy-two hours without sleeping because I grew paranoid that, if I fell asleep, I would stop breathing.

Before you accuse me of having no faith, let me note that I have lived in and walked by faith for nearly all my life. I have seen extraordinary miracles and supernatural breakthroughs across the globe. But in my *this* moment of crisis, pain, and fear, I was reminded that my faith does not have to keep me from the fire to be true faith. I will never pretend I was unafraid, but I will never forget that even when the fear was real, so was my faith.

I never blamed God for my situation. He is too good

to do harm to His child, but He did allow *this*. I determined to keep trusting Him, to believe His Word, and to stand on His promises rather than complain. This formula for overcoming is not limited to when you have an evil virus in your body. These foundational truths will get you through any *this* season.

"You are going to die." Was it my inner voice speaking, or was the enemy whispering these gloomy thoughts? "You are never going to see your girls get married. Your wife is going to raise the kids alone. It is over. You messed up and got sick. Now your family is going to be left without you."

I was dehydrated. I was delirious. I thought I was dying. It was a dark place, and I have no problem telling you that I never want to experience that again. But even as the darkness surrounded me, my faith began to stir.

On the morning of the tenth day, I remained separated from my family to keep them from exposure. I slowly crawled out of my bed, walked to our big mahogany front door, and mustered all my strength to open it.

"I shall live and not die and declare the works of the Lord!" I yelled aloud out the door. "I command in the name of Jesus every foul spirit of fear and death to leave this house!"

If you are wondering if I suddenly felt better or if a warm sensation of being healed shot through my body, the answer is no. I felt none of those things. In fact, I was so weak and had yelled so loudly that I almost passed out. But I let the enemy know that I refused to listen to his loud mouth without being loud back.

James tells us there is power in resisting the devil

(Jas. 4:7). I knew I had to change the atmosphere in my house, so I turned on a song by my friend Eddie James. As "Holy Spirit" played throughout my house, something happened in the unseen realm. Although I did not feel a lot different (I literally crawled back into bed), something happened. Lines had been drawn.

The next night during our midweek service, my brother-in-law, our outreach pastor, stopped his sermon and called the church to pray for me. Miles away at my home, I felt a shift in my body while I lay in bed. When they prayed at church, God touched me in my home. I was coming out of *this*!

After twenty-one days of wrestling with this fiendish virus, God delivered me. A pulmonologist told me to be prepared for a six-to-eight-week recovery, but the kindness of God shrank that prediction. In a few weeks, I returned to the pulpit with the anointing of God strengthening me for my assignment.

FOR OUR STRENGTH AND HIS GLORY

It is easy to lose the personal stories in the big picture of the pandemic. But for me, it was an unforgettable season. And although I would never want to experience that sickness again, I am stronger because God allowed me to come through it.

I believe my experience with COVID-19 is a microcosm of a *this* season that God's people have experienced both individually and corporately. You may not have wrestled with this particular disease. Maybe you did and you had no symptoms. (If so, you ought to give God an extra praise today!) But all of us can testify that at some point in our journeys we have wrestled with a chapter, a season, a *this* that we had to fight our way through. Nobody gets a free pass that exempts us from *this*. You either have faced or you will face *this* eventually.

When we are going through turbulence, we love to have someone to blame. Somehow, it seems easier for us to navigate in it if we can find a target for our disdain at being faced with such difficulty. The pandemic has been no different. Many have engaged in unfruitful and unending arguments about who was responsible for *this*. For me, to jump into the fray seeking an answer to the "who did this" question would be a waste of time. As with many situations, we do not have all the answers, and we probably never will. While origins of *this* may be beyond my ability to know, I unequivocally believe that God uses every *this* situation for His glory and our good. His kingdom will advance, and His people will see victory. If the Bible reveals anything about our faith journey, it is that perseverance wins, no matter what *this* is.

THE EFFECT ON THE CHURCH

This seasons can be felt on both macro and micro levels of Christianity. Although we have been talking about the micro level of *this* seasons in the lives of individual believers, the macro-level effects are the result of both an accumulated experience of individuals and the corporate experience of the body as a unique organism. So *this* seasons can affect the whole church.

On the macro level, as I write this book, the universal

church is exiting its most defining *this* moment in a generation. Never in modern history has the rhythm of life been as disrupted as it was during *this*—a worldwide season of sickness and uncertainty. No matter your political affiliation, position, or persuasion, *this* pandemic has been the most disruptive intrusion into our daily lives since the world wars. Like every generational defining moment, the effects linger. We are still discovering where we go from here.

"I don't know" is not a phrase that leaders like to use. We like to show certainty about where we are headed, but *this* has left no room for that. I took numerous calls during the pandemic in which pastors or leaders asked for help with strategies about how to lead during *this* period of unknowns. No detailed blueprint existed. We experienced an anomaly. When you go where no one else has gone before, you do not get the luxury of breaking open the map and following the path blazed by others. You become the leader.

God uses these inimitable situations in our lives to break our dependence on other things. We have so many books, websites, and peer groups to rely on that sometimes we neglect to follow the Holy Spirit. *This* seasons do not allow for that. Your hope of coming through *this* is tied directly to your willingness to depend on and follow the Holy Spirit. You must pull out the ancient compass and just keep moving in the right direction, following God's voice, though it be but a whisper.

God has the right to keep sovereign secrets. Although some prophesied the general idea of a coming pandemic, the outbreak of COVID-19 was unexpected. Its shocking arrival exposed the church's lack in many areas. I am no church basher, but let's be honest: we needed to be checked. The Western church had evolved, or devolved, into a murky alloy, a diluted mixture, of what God intended.

My goal is not caustic belligerence, but I had already observed an unhealthy trifecta developing in the Western church. First, there was a growing tolerance of sin. Second, I noticed a reduction in biblical, expository preaching of truth. Finally, our worship gatherings became more about nickels, noses, and numbers and less about worshipping Jesus and life-changing encounters with His presence.

The church's arrival at *this* came from a perfect storm of taking the wrong actions and then measuring by the wrong metrics. When we are doing things wrong but getting "great" results (crowds and cash), it is a recipe for disaster. It reminds me of sitting in a burning home and telling yourself you are going to be OK because you have a water faucet in the kitchen and a beautiful decorating scheme on the walls. It is absurd. It is dangerous. And it is where we are.

Even as my heart was stirred by my observations, I found myself wondering how the church could ever be checked and challenged at a global level. It is hard enough to have reckoning and repentance in a single congregation, and it may rarely happen in a whole city. But what it would take for the church in an entire hemisphere or even the whole world to be stirred from slumber was almost beyond my comprehension. Then, seemingly out of nowhere, COVID-19 burst onto the scene. I went from wondering how change could possibly touch every congregation to noticing something so widespread that I do not know of a congregation that was not impacted in some way.

The COVID reality check caused me to pause and assess myself and my church. At the Spirit's direction, I found myself retreating to the Book of Acts quite frequently during the pandemic. Though I tried to follow the Spirit's prompting, I also found myself comforted by a book of the Bible filled with firsts for the church. Whether it was the first outpouring of God's Spirit, the first adversity, the first church quarrels, the selection of the first missionaries for the first mission trip or deacons for the first deacon board (some wish it would have been the last!), Acts is a textbook in handling firsts. While their terrain may have been different from ours, a strategy for handling the unknowns and unexpected can be found in the pages of Acts.

THE HOLY SPIRIT, NOT ANSWERS

In Acts, we do not find lots of examples of God giving the early church step-by-step instructions of how to do everything. Even in the Gospels, Jesus was not heavy on detailed information. He talked about relationship and intimacy with the Father. He did not provide a cheap map that showed the *way* without the traveler knowing the *Way* (John 14:6). Intimacy with God and walking in the Spirit got them through every new *this* the church faced.

Even though we know the unexpected is inevitable, no one likes a surprise *this*. We prefer receiving a heavy download of inside information that prevents us from that feeling of vulnerability. Even the apostles wanted to know what was coming their way. They often asked Jesus questions regarding the future to help them navigate the unfamiliar and unsettling land of the unknown. They were especially interested in when the kingdom of Israel would be restored.

Observe this account in Acts chapter 1, which is a conversation Jesus has with His disciples after the resurrection and just before He ascends to heaven.

> So when they had come together, they asked Him, "Lord, will You at this time restore the kingdom to Israel?" He said to them, "It is not for you to know the times or the dates, which the Father has fixed by His own authority. But you shall receive power when the Holy Spirit comes upon you. And you shall be My witnesses in Jerusalem, and in all Judea and Samaria, and to the ends of the earth."
>
> —ACTS 1:6–8, MEV

Though His followers wanted insight regarding the future, Jesus never hands them details and dates. On the contrary, He rebukes their infatuation with foreknowledge and tells them they should not be concerned with the details of the future. Yet even though Jesus does not give them what they ask, He does not leave the disciples empty-handed. He gives them something much better than a juicy download of inside information—the promise that the power of God will be available and that the world will hear the gospel of Jesus because of their witness. He points them beyond their meager request to a promise that would prepare them for a glorious invasion of the Holy Spirit and a forthcoming experience of power that would make them the devil's worst nightmare.

On one hand, Jesus tells them they will not know every detail and date regarding the future. Yet He promises them the Holy Spirit, who will guide them into all truth and teach them all things. It is not for us to know the times and seasons, but we are going to receive the Spirit, who knows and reveals all things. Process that paradox. Further, it is the Holy Spirit who reveals the heart and revelations of the Father.

> But as it is written, "Eye has not seen, nor ear heard, nor has it entered into the heart of man the things which God has prepared for those who love Him." But God has revealed them to us by His Spirit. For the Spirit searches all things, yes, the deep things of God.
>
> —1 CORINTHIANS 2:9–10, MEV

We find ourselves living in this tension: though we are instructed against seeking dates and details, we have One living in us who knows all things. I have concluded that while we may not know the times and epochs before they happen, the Father certainly wants us to be able to discern them as they unfold. Furthermore, clarity is only accomplished by relying on the Holy Spirit no matter which *this* shows up in our lives. God in His absolute mercy refuses to make this journey so easy that we could do it without relying on Him.

The COVID-19 pandemic, while being the most difficult

experience this generation has ever walked through, also has created unimaginable opportunities for the church. For one, we immediately discovered the need for and power of a social media footprint. Digital delivery of the gospel wasn't just an option for the technologically savvy; it became the mode of communication for thousands of leaders as we dealt with the global disease. From my vantage point, I also saw communities lean on the church during the crisis. While I recognize that there were some locales that attempted to keep the church "shut down" and at arm's length from the people, I also watched as pastors leveraged their buildings and property to cooperate with their local leaders to provide testing, child care, food distribution, and other needed services.

Finally, I think the pandemic pressured us into resourcefulness and creativity. I personally sensed an opportunity to return to organic, relational connectivity in the midst of the crisis. I think we had gotten so big-church-oriented that many had to scramble to keep people and mission together. It was almost as if there was a collective moan among those in the kingdom since our big buildings and stages had been emptied and silenced. I felt an urgency to make sure we returned to the roots of the early church movement.

In fact, during a team meeting with our leaders, I told them that we needed to pandemic-proof our church for the future. God forbid this travesty ever be repeated, but in the event that something happened beyond our control or wishes, our church needed to create a template of operation that could be built in homes among friends and remain evangelistic in nature. I wanted to make sure we provided strategies for fellowship, prayer, and discipleship. In short, no virus or entity should ever be able to shut the church down or put it out of business. And many leaders had to think creatively about methods and means to keep the church on its mission to advance the kingdom rather than simply react to the daily dose of doom and gloom.

How the church responded to *this* season of pandemic and the truths we learned would determine much about her future. I decided to press into the Holy Spirit in a greater way because I knew He had something in mind. There is a *next* beyond the chaos of this current state of confusion, and whatever God was doing after *this,* I wanted to be part of it.

FACING *THIS* WITH JOY

This was not unique for the early church, and *this* is not unique to the modern church. All of us must deal with *this* seasons. From Genesis to Revelation, patriarchs and matriarchs of the faith wrestled with *this,* and the way they handled those moments left their marks on the faith.

After murdering an Egyptian for beating a Hebrew slave (Exod. 2:11), Moses descended from hero to goatherd in a twenty-four-hour period. But that was not his last round of *this.* Almost before the blood of the Passover lamb had dried on the doorposts of Egypt, the complaining Israelites decided that Moses, who led them out of captivity in

Egypt, was not the leader they wanted to lead them into the Promised Land.

Job may be the most often cited example of *this*. Imagine living in the favor and blessings of God only to be informed that suddenly your fortune has changed. You are now childless, penniless, and friendless (Job 1). Daniel's *this* was a den of angry lions into which he was thrown for praying to the Lord his God (Dan. 6:16). David had to deal with *this* uncircumcised Philistine giant (1 Sam. 17:26). Mary had to deal with *this* when she got sideways looks walking through town in her third trimester after claiming that she had never been intimate with Joseph. She alone knew her womb was filled with the Child of promise (Luke 1:35).

Lazarus had to deal with *this* sickness (John 11:1). Jesus had to drink from *this* cup (Matt. 26:39). Peter had to deal with *this* failure of denying the Lord. You cannot read the Scriptures without seeing one encounter after another with *this*. The concept of an inconvenient, interrupting, unknown *this* is even seen in the Book of Revelation with John being exiled and alone, dealing with *this* on an isle called Patmos, all so he could tell the church that another *this* was coming (Rev. 1:9).

If you close your Bible and look around, you will see that the mess of *this* did not end with those witnesses in Scripture. We can all testify about a *this* in our own lives. For some it may start out with *this* tumor. For another, it is recovering from *this* divorce. Some of you are trying to resurrect a ministry that is on life support after dealing with the carnage of COVID-19. What is your *this*? Is it a bankruptcy? A failed business deal? A miscarriage? It could be a marriage *this*, a money *this*, a ministry *this*, or a mental *this*. Whatever the *this*, we are all faced with the question, "What is *this*, and what do I do with it?"

You fight through the tears. You collect yourself and try to hide the pain and frustration raging on the inside. Whether the wounds are old or new, their pain is still fresh because it is still *this*. It is not a distant *that* or *then*; it is an ever-present, ever-hurting, always-with-you *this*. No matter how long ago it happened and how removed from the event you may be, it is still a *this*. It is within reach. It is present.

Friend, no matter the depths of your *this*, a greater *this* is on the way for you. You will not stay stuck in the storm. You are not banished to wander in some wilderness. Resist the feeling that joy and peace are only awaiting you in some nebulous place at a mysterious time beyond the end of your days.

> I believe I will see the goodness of the Lord in the land of the living. Wait on the Lord; be strong, and may your heart be stout; wait on the Lord.
>
> —Psalm 27:13–14, MEV

Yes, we will find joy unsurpassed when we reach our reward, but the text does not suggest you have to wait until heaven to find joy. Growing up we sang, "Everybody Will Be Happy Over There." To be clear, I will most assuredly get happy when we get over there, but joy is the privileged portion for the saints while living in the nasty now.

Grab that truth in the midst of your struggle. You have every right to believe you will experience His blessing right in the middle of *this*!

Whatever you have experienced in the land of the living, I want you to muster all the strength you can and declare, "I believe I will see the goodness of God in the land of the living!"

One reason for doing this is that your *this* has a purpose.

CHAPTER 3

This Is Just a Test

DURING MY TIME in ministry, I have been blessed to meet some amazing people from a variety of backgrounds. Thousands of miles in airplanes, stays in hundreds of hotels, and countless conversations with restaurant wait staff, not to mention encounters at church fellowships and in green rooms, plus precious moments spent with God's people lingering to talk a few moments after a revival service—all these have given me a wide sampling of humanity. One thing rings true among all the people I have encountered: no matter their socioeconomic status, ethnicity, church affiliation, or any other identifier, all people have walked their unique journeys and have perspectives solely their own.

We all view life through our personal lens. Each of us has a worldview shaped by our particular journey. We can view the same thing or hear the same words and still come away with different conclusions simply because we respond from our individual perspectives. The danger is that we can end up thinking we are being objective when we are actually being subjective, and that can lead to all sorts of wrong conclusions.

Subjective observations can be damaging in some situations, but none are more destructive than when we approach Scripture. I recognize that we are inclined to personal bias, so I take special care not to bend the text in my direction when I am studying the Bible. I do not want to manipulate the text inaccurately to accommodate my situation or circumstances.

The beautiful thing is that we never need to misinterpret the Bible to find something that fits where we are. The Bible contains enough Word that you will always be able to find something that addresses your situation if you study it. Read the Bible. Let the Bible read you. As you dive into the Word, God will take a text and make it a *rhema* word for just where you are. In those moments, the words jump off the page and become God's expressed and direct word to you. Your faith explodes. A spirit of wisdom and revelation come. Your eyes are opened and what previously seemed inaccessible and unworkable suddenly becomes reality.

"THAT WAS A TEST"

The story of Abraham and Isaac in Genesis chapter 22 became such a text for me. Isaac was the child God promised Abraham, even though he and his wife were old and she was past her child-bearing years. After Abraham believed God for over two decades, God fulfilled His promise and Isaac was born.

I will tell you what God showed me about Abraham, but first you must know that my default position is go, especially when it comes to kingdom matters. Drifting through life is not for me. I maintain a ready posture, poised and prepared to move forward. So during the year of COVID, when all the activity stopped with what sometimes felt like progress-killing lockdowns, quarantines, and safety measures, I was having a difficult time staying still. I was ready to *go*, but everything was yelling *stop*. Like many other ministry leaders, I spent a lot of 2020 frustrated over the feeling that advancement had been halted.

Later, as I looked back over that year, I thought, "What was that?" I wanted to be sure I had not missed something valuable amid all the difficulties. I found myself thinking there had to be some biblical explanation to the question "What in the world did I just come out of? What was that?"

When I do not have clarity on something, I turn to prayer. So I asked the Lord, "Father, can You help me understand what that was? What was 2020?"

"That was a test."

When the Holy Ghost whispered that response into my spirit, a conglomeration of recollections, both painful and sweet, took shape in my mind. Uncertainties, loss of friends, change in operational paradigms, and even my own encounter with COVID—all these came rushing back. For a moment, I was awed by just how momentous that season had been—not just for me, but for all of us. As I processed the facts and feelings, I was nudged by the Spirit to go to Genesis chapter 22. There I rediscovered the testing of Abraham.

GOD TESTED ABRAHAM

Abraham's story is not a new one to most believers, and certainly not to preachers. Though I have taught the truths found in his story before, this time I was reading the text with new eyes. Like you, this season had molded my understanding in fresh ways. With my new perspective and the guidance of the Holy Spirit, the familiar story yielded fresh revelation.

Reading through the passage, I was struck by how familiar this test felt to me. As I mentioned in the previous chapter, we are like the believers of the New Testament: we want to know details. We do not just want to know what God is doing; we want to know why and how, and we usually want to know right now. But God works in ways that are not always clear to us. Have you ever gone through something with God but without all the details? Abraham was about to go through an experience without any of the details or answers.

After Isaac was born, Genesis 22:1 reports, "After these things God tested Abraham" (NRSV). God asked Abraham to sacrifice Isaac, the child through whom Abraham would become the father of nations and through whom all of God's promises to him would be fulfilled.

You and I read this story with the advantage of hindsight. We have the privilege of knowing *this* was a test from God. But without the benefit of knowing what God was up to, I wonder what it felt like to Abraham. A little test?

No. For him, *this* was hell on earth. We have the privilege of knowing the end of the matter, but Abraham knew nothing of the sort. This is one of the most famous tests of faith in all of literature, and Abraham is in the middle of it. He is not an onlooker, and he has no secret information informing him that God is testing him. Abraham is walking by faith.

It never ceases to amaze me how much more clearly we can see other folk's situations than our own. When you are in the middle of a test, everybody knows exactly what to say, and they all have so much faith—at least for your problems. In an attempt to encourage you, people say churchy things.

"It's going to be OK."

"Tie a knot in the rope and hang on!"

Or, my favorite, "If you could see what God was doing, you would understand."

Oh, so you mean all I must do is gain a perfect understanding of what the omnipotent, omniscient, sovereign God of the universe is doing? No problem! Why was I even worried? If only it were that easy.

Notice how Genesis 22:1 begins: "After these things" (NRSV). Those words are profound. I thought some of the things he already walked through had been tests. Imagine God interrupting your comfortable life to tell you He has a place for you to go but not letting you in on where, when, and how you are going to get there. Would that be a test? What if a family member were kidnapped in a raid led by several kings, and you were the one who had to lead the rescue party. Feeling tested yet? Imagine being promised a son and then having to wait twenty-five years before he was born. Would that feel like a test? Yet the text is clear that this test came after those things.

Abraham discovered that the test was not only waiting for Isaac to be born but also being willing to trust God when He asked him to sacrifice his boy. This moment is going to show us something about tests. Your navigation of spiritual tests will not be defined by their degree of *difficulty* but by your degree of *dependency*. As the story unfolds, we discover that God was not in pursuit of Isaac's life. Instead, He was confirming that He had Abraham's heart. Can you depend on the faithfulness of God, no matter the cost? What about when it does not make sense? Do you still trust God? This was Abraham's test.

As I followed the Holy Spirit and took more time to think about this test, it became clear that this is where the church had been during COVID. We were navigating a test of our faith in God and our dependency upon Him.

I made a commitment to speak candidly regarding my experience during COVID, including what God was speaking to me. So let me be transparent. It seemed that many moments in 2020 came to destroy my joy. I am a pastor; I hate being away from my people. That season was hard. Additionally, the social unrest in our nation became an issue I had to deal with personally. Perhaps it is a good time to tell you that I believe kingdom leaders ought to passionately engage the culture and address issues that are prevalent in our world. If we are silent, Satan will speak and the spirit of this age will educate our children. We have to select those moments carefully, but some hills, as the old saying indicates, are worth dying on.

In 2020 I felt as if my death on those hills were almost literal. There were times when I had to speak against injustice. There were times when I had to walk with African American brothers and sisters in solidarity and compassion as we dealt with the aftermath of unnecessary death in our streets. There were moments when we loved and cared for children abandoned at the border. Those engagements and others brought both expected and unexpected consequences.

From being threatened for doing all I could to bring healing to our community to being castigated for going to the border to witness the conditions of children being kept in detention facilities, at times 2020 felt like war. The threats were so serious I literally went to bed with a policeman in front of my home because the authorities had determined my life could be in danger. Our church drew criticism for walking out the most basic tenets of Christian faith. Sometimes the enemy told me I was going to die. If I tried to tell you that I enjoyed every moment of that year, I would be lying. Some of the things we go through in life will never be enjoyable.

Maybe you enjoyed tests when you were growing up. I did not. I would have almost preferred a trip to the dentist for a root canal to taking a test. I even had a tremendous dislike for anyone who gave me a test.

As I matured, I realized that tests were useful, that their purpose was not to hold someone back. Of course, I did have some friends who would swear otherwise! They were convinced that our high school algebra teacher gave tests for the sole purpose of halting our progress. But in reality, tests were assessments that determined whether or not we had retained sufficient knowledge to qualify for advancement to the next level. No matter our feelings about them, tests are simply assessments.

TESTS REVEAL CHARACTER

Apply that understanding to where you are now. Recognize that the test you have been going through was never meant to hold you back. In fact, it was not even meant to teach you anything. The test proves the content of your character, the essence of your identity, and the extent of your obedience to God. The test was not given to Abraham to torment him; it was given to prove what was within him. You will never know the substance of your soul and the content of your own spirit until you are put under pressure and observe what is squeezed out.

Without a test, your testimony is suspect. The pressures of life and the anguish of struggles take inventory of what is in your heart. You can say you are a man or woman of faith. You can impress your peers with bold proclamations, but the test will reveal the reality. Your test is not an assassination; it is an evaluation.

The test of awareness

The first test of Abraham's character involved the test of awareness. God called Abraham by name. When God called him, Abraham had to be cognizant that the Almighty was talking to Him.

I know firsthand about failing this test miserably. I was sitting in an airport waiting for my flight to board. I knew the scheduled time of departure, and I had found a seat in the waiting area nearest to my gate. All I had to do was listen for my section of the plane to be called, and I would be off to preach in a distant city. I had prayed and prepared for the service, and I had a word burning in my heart. I was excited for the trip. Yet when they called for my section, there I sat, headphones on, my favorite prayer playlist playing in my ears. They called, but I did not move because I could not hear the call. Even though they called my name several times, I was listening to something else.

I missed my flight. There I sat, preparing my heart for the night's assignment, but with no way to get there. I was in the right place at the right time, but I still missed my opportunity because I was not aware of my name being called. Thankfully, by the grace of God and the kindness of a ticket agent, I caught the next flight and made it to my engagement that night. However, I learned a valuable lesson: you must be aware when you are being called.

If we are not careful, we can miss it when God calls our name because of the many distractions that vie for our attention. Our careers, hobbies, entertainment, or even things that are close to our calling distract us from the voice of God. If Abraham were going to become a father of many nations, then he must at the very minimum pass the test of awareness. Likewise, you have to know when God is talking to you. Otherwise, you just might miss your moment.

We get distracted when, even for just a moment, we are more interested in something else than God. Are you attentive to what is happening in His kingdom? Do not miss the moments when God is calling you. Your purpose and calling go beyond anything you have dreamed. But it is connected to your ability to hear God call your name! When God speaks, will you pass the awareness test?

The test of availability

The second test Abraham encountered was the test of availability. If God wants to use someone, He has to find someone who is available. I did not say *able*; I said *available*. Be careful that you do not esteem ability above availability. Do not misunderstand me. Ability and giftedness are important tools in the journey. Never doubt that God will equip you to fulfill your calling. Yet too many times we rely on our abilities and avoid the high cost of availability.

You may have never considered that availability could have a cost because you view availability as having nothing else on your schedule. That is not the kind of availability that attracts God. He wants your intentional availability.

When God called Abraham to sacrifice his son, Abraham responded positively with the Hebrew word *hineni*. Isaiah used this same Hebrew word when God asked him, "Who will go for Us?" *Hineni* is the ultimate response to display availability when God calls on you. It literally means, "Here I am, at Your service, Lord! What do You need?"[1]

Let me meddle a bit. If the Lord says, "I need a preacher, singer, or someone to take the stage with a microphone," many are quick to respond, "*Hineni*!" Yet when God needs a parking lot attendant, a small group teacher, a greeter, or an intercessor, I wonder how many are so available?

God is growing tired of people putting a premium on

being in the spotlight but not being a servant. When we reach the point where we are more concerned about what we get out of it than what we are actually doing in ministry, we are in trouble. Sadly, the church finds itself more concerned with stage time and chasing social media clout than being in the middle of what God is doing. Far too many who ought to be serving in the shadows are instead in pursuit of accolades, derailed from their calling by their addiction to applause. This narcissistic approach to kingdom business has shifted attention from the Creator to creation and is an enemy of real revival.

"Here I am, at Your service" should be our motto, even without knowing all the details and certainly without concern for what we are set to gain personally. Remember the encounter the rich, young ruler had with Jesus in Mark 10:17–27. Jesus invited him on the adventure of a lifetime, but he failed the test of availability. The church calls him the rich, young ruler, but I call him the poor, immature slave. How can you be a ruler if you are enslaved to your possessions instead of mastering them? When God calls, will you only hear, or will you be able to heed? Are you available?

The test of alignment

The next test in the Genesis 22 story is the test of alignment. Before Abraham experienced the miraculous provision of God, he aligned himself with God's will and purpose for him. He recognized that the journey up the mountain to sacrifice Isaac would be filled with exit ramps—chances for people to abandon God's plan.

Remember, Abraham took his son, two other young men, and a donkey on this journey. The two lads came with him for part of the journey, but they had to exit the entourage at the mountain and wait for Abraham to return from the summit. They would not travel to the top of the mountain. They would not be there for the climax of the test. They would not see God's incredible grace in action.

You may have already experienced something similar in your climb. During the biggest struggles of your life, when you were on your way to conquering insurmountable odds, some folks left you. I want you to know that you will be OK without them. You may have wanted them to keep climbing with you, but too many people can become a liability in your pursuit of all that God has for you. As you ascend, your circle will shrink. Do not panic. Let God align you with His will. He knows the people you need. We are much better at believing God knows *what* we need than *whom* we need. But He knows, and we must trust Him.

Abraham had to look at the lads and tell them that they could not go where he was going. When this happens to you, the enemy will tell you that you are being alienated and abandoned, and that their departure is a sign of your failure. Do not listen to that lie!

There is a difference between alienation and separation. Alienation happens when they leave you. Separation happens when you look at your purpose and destiny and realize that you value those too highly to hang with people who are keeping you from what God put you on this planet to pursue. So, to become everything God called you to be, He aligns you with His purposes alone.

The sure sign of an alignment season is when familiar faces become distant. In alignment, people who traveled with you to that point cannot travel with you up that hill. They may have been your friends. But alignment is not a test of companionship; it is a test of capacity and calling. They may not be called where you are going, and that is OK. If they are not, they certainly will not be able to handle what you will find when you get there.

Abraham responded to this test by telling the young men that he and his boy were going on to worship. Did you catch that? They were going to worship!

God is looking for people who will be separated, not through arrogant isolation, but to spend some time with Him in worship. I am going yonder to worship. You can stay in the valley with the donkeys if you want, but I have too much on the line. I am going to worship.

When encountering God becomes your priority, alignment is much easier to handle.

The test of accessibility

Not only was Abraham available to God, but he was also accessible to Isaac. If we fail the test of accessibility, we hinder the fulfillment of God's plan in our generation. Argue His sovereignty all you want, but we cannot abdicate our responsibility. We are commissioned again and again to point the next generation to Jesus.

The Bible often refers to our heavenly Father as the God of Abraham, Isaac, and Jacob. In practicality, that is because Abraham shared his God experiences with Isaac, and Isaac shared his God experiences with Jacob. A spiritual legacy occurs when fathers tap into the power of accessibility. We should constantly be reaching in two directions: toward God, to reach Him, and toward sons and daughters, to help them know God as we do. This cannot happen if we are not accessible.

This theme of accessibility crescendos when Isaac asks his father, "Where is the lamb?" (Gen. 22:7). What a powerful representation of eternal truth! Isaac asked his dad that question. But I hear the roar of a younger generation walking the earth in my day, and they too are asking, "Where is the Lamb?"

We hear a generation crying out, "We have everything we need: fire, wood, smoke machines, lights, click tracks, bells, whistles, and megachurch accoutrements. But where is the Lamb?"

Stop telling yourself that this younger generation is looking for a show in church. They are looking for the Lamb! These are sincere sons and daughters who have recognized that there is more to the kingdom than the anemic "churchianity" many of them have inherited. They will not settle for systems, structures, and religiosity. They will not be satisfied until they have experienced the depths of who Jesus is. They want the Lamb. Will we help them find Him?

They are seeking access to fathers who can lead them to Jesus. They will push away the constructs of men and flee from systems that are self-serving. They will quickly move past clichés and church lingo. They will not be satisfied with sermons hastily downloaded on Saturday evening, and they will balk at shallow worship. They are not here for church as we know it; they are here for the Lamb! They will not stop until they see eyes like fire, hair like wool, feet like brass, and a voice like the sound of many waters (Rev. 1:14–15).

I do not know about you, but I am tired of coming to church and leaving not knowing where the Lamb was. I am going to echo father Abraham when he came to a point in the journey and declared to Isaac his younger son, "God will provide himself a lamb" (Gen. 22:8, KJV).

Let me declare to all the hungry, thirsty, God-chasing, Holy-Spirit-desiring, tired-of-the-usual, ready-for-more, Jesus-seeking people who are reading these words: you will not be disappointed. The Lamb you have been looking for has been provided. He is available, and if you seek Him, you will find Him. Do not buy into some watered-down experience. Do not be discouraged by Sister Flip-Flop and Brother Flim-Flam, who have been convinced that a move of God is a thing of the past. Those around you may believe that dismal report, but whatever you do, do not give up on the Lamb. There is a Christ-centered, Spirit-empowered awakening coming to the earth, and you are going to be in the middle of it!

The test of the altar

The final test Abraham encountered was perhaps the most critical of all. In the test of the altar, he offered his promised child to God to become a burnt offering. His son was on the altar. His promised boy was about to die.

He was moments away from being the man who sacrificed his child in radical obedience to God.

If you read this text as a story of a man almost taking the life of his son, you may think that God is a bit morbid and that Abraham is a lot crazy. But if you read the eleventh chapter of Hebrews, you will discover that Abraham is not crazy and God is not morbid. Those verses reveal Abraham's thought process as he prepared to sacrifice his son on an altar.

> By faith Abraham, when he was tested, offered up Isaac, and he who had received the promises offered up his only begotten son, of whom it was said, "In Isaac your seed shall be called," concluding that God was able to raise him up, even from the dead, from which he also received him in a figurative sense.
>
> —HEBREWS 11:16–19

Did you catch that? Abraham did not see this moment as *murder* in the making. He saw it as a *miracle* in the making! Abraham was not just a man of obedience but also a man of faith. We do not call him the father of obedience; we call him the father of our faith. Why? Because Abraham believed that if he took Isaacs's life, God would do something on that mountain that had never been done: He would literally raise Isaac from the dead.

Abraham had the kind of faith that was needed to pass the altar test. He knew that God could be trusted with even his most precious possessions, dreams, and hopes. Remember, although Abraham had no understanding of how God would do it, he demonstrated total faith and trust in God. His obedience unlocked his destiny.

The greatest blessing and breakthrough you will ever experience in your life will come when you pass this test by placing what is most precious to you on the altar. God has power to bring back to life that which has died. If I lose everything, if He takes it all away, He is good enough and God enough to restore all that I put on the altar.

Perhaps your journey has taken you to a place like Abraham's mountain of sacrifice. You have heard God's voice and obeyed it. Along the way, some people have left your circle, but you have been single-minded in your pursuit of God. Yet you find yourself feeling like you are paying a cost that you never imagined. Yes, you want to walk in obedience and faith, but what on earth is happening? Some precious things seem as if they are about to die.

Let me remind you, there is resurrection power on the mountain. In the middle of your mess, in the middle of your trial, in the middle of the hell you are walking through, help is on the way! This is not a murder; it is a miracle.

The test you have just come through, or maybe even the one you are in now, is not designed to kill you but to reveal you. God is about to show you His glory on the top of the mountain.

God said to Abraham, "Now I know" (Gen. 22:12).

When God sees you lay what is precious on the altar, it will be as if He says, "Now I know...."

People will often condemn your harvest because they

did not see your seed. They do not understand that the only reason you have a right mind and a suit on is because you have the Lord! They never saw that you passed tests that left you holding nothing, that you laid what was precious on the altar, and that only the goodness of God put these blessings in your hand.

God saw that Abraham was willing to sacrifice all, so He provided a substitute sacrifice for Isaac in the form of a ram that was caught in a thicket (Gen. 22:13). God used that bush to tie up that ram by the horns until Abraham arrived and needed it. When Abraham successfully passed the test, he experienced God's supernatural provision.

Let me close this chapter by encouraging you. I feel the unction to tell you that God knows how to tie up your blessing until you are ready for it. Family, it is time to take what Christ died to give you! He tied it up for you. He tied that miracle up for you. It cannot get away. He tied that healing up for you. Be healed now in Jesus' name! That blessing, that breakthrough, is tied up for you. It cannot get away. You have no need to lose sleep over it. It has your name on it. It is tied up!

Do not miss this. While God is the only One who can tie up your blessing, you are the only one who can take it! God has it on reserve for you. Take your healing! Take your miracle! Take your blessing! Take your liberty! God has provided.

Your test came for one purpose, to assess your readiness for advancement. When you depend on the strength of God and press in to Him in the moments of testing and trial, you can testify like Job, "But He knows the way that I take; when He has tested me, I shall come forth as gold" (Job 23:10).

God tests us to advance us, even during times of adversity.

CHAPTER 4

Advance in Adversity

LIKE MANY OF you, my family and I enjoy getting away periodically so we can spend time together and make great memories. I recently took a trip with my family, Mom and Dad, and my sister and her children. We went to the quaint mountain town of Pigeon Forge, Tennessee, to spend time with my nephew who was about to leave us for army boot camp.

Christmastime in Pigeon Forge is magical. There tucked in the hills and hollers of east Tennessee you will find Dollywood, where cotton candy is king, funnel cakes abound, and high-tech carnival rides await. Everywhere you go, you hear the screams of ladies and gentlemen losing their voices on wooden roller coasters that race through the forests of the Great Smoky Mountains. Sometime during all this fun, I watched my mother buckle under pressure from her grandchildren and get on a roller-coaster-style ride. I had never seen her ride anything like that before. It was called the Barnstormer, and the grandkids persuaded her to believe it was just a giant swing (called the Barnstormer!). Riders travel progressively higher on each swing of the Barnstormer's massive arms, reaching a maximum speed of 45 miles per hour and achieving 230 degrees of rotation. At its peak, the Barnstormer goes 81 feet in the air! And my mom agreed to get on.

When her ride was finished, my sweet mother stumbled off the Barnstormer with her hair as multidirectional as if she had been standing in a hurricane. She could not walk a straight line and she was weak-kneed. My dad put his arms under hers and assisted her up, attempting to help her salvage any similitude of dignity that she had remaining.

I immediately went to work on the PR side of things, making sure the grandkids had not jeopardized any inheritance they were expecting. Some people go to Dollywood for the rides. Some grandchildren go in hopes of deceiving their grandmother into riding a machine that leaves her looking like she got into a fight with a hedge trimmer.

But I did not go to Dollywood for the rides. I went to Dollywood for the lights. When we entered the park, an employee reminded us that at Christmastime, Dollywood boasts five million lights throughout the park. To make sure we got to see the lights, I asked one of the workers about it.

"Pardon me, ma'am. When do the lights come on here at the park?"

"The lights are on all day, but they don't show up until it gets dark."

When I heard that, I nearly pulled out my wallet to give her an offering for the revelation she had unknowingly dropped in my spirit. The lights are not turned off at Dollywood. They are simply not seen until it is dark.

This is a truth for the church. While we are to shine all the time, it isn't until the darkness comes that we are seen most clearly. We thrive in darkness! The problem is that many times we want to wait until the darkness passes before we shine. I get the impression we are waiting for political alignment, legislation, and an end to global turbulence before we believe it is our turn. I want to announce that it is our turn right now. Darkness may be an enemy, but it is also a terrific backdrop against which the light of God's church can be seen.

You may be tempted to believe that all the adversity the early church encountered gave them permission to complain and stop the forward progress of Christ's agenda. The sympathetic side of my soul wants to believe that God would exempt them from their kingdom assignment and responsibilities, even with a short reprieve. You might even assume that the challenges they faced made moving the gospel forward in their generation too difficult. Nothing could be further from the truth.

The Bible teaches us a powerful principle that today's church needs to get a revelation on. We must advance the kingdom even in the midst of adversity. This is not a statement of possibility; it is a statement of reality. In order for us to seize the moment we are living in, the church must get accustomed to thriving in hostility and advancing the purposes of God in the earth, even when the enemy shows up to resist us.

I am concerned that we have been fed an unhealthy diet of "resistance-free" gospel. Too many saints wilt like flowers in a July drought when the heat of adversity is turned up. Frankly, it is embarrassing how quickly we contemplate surrender.

I believe completely in victory, in the promise and the power of breakthrough (this is coming in the next chapter). I have rejoiced every time the Lord has graciously given us a breakthrough in our circumstances. Furthermore, I am glad that weeping and sorrow only endure for a night. A morning is coming that will extinguish the heat of hopelessness that tries to rob us of our season. But I think we need to be reminded that, even as we wait for joy to arrive, we can stand in faith, operate on the offensive, and move the agenda of the Lamb forward.

MULTIPLICATION IN AFFLICTION

Remember Acts chapter 8? The church was being persecuted and the furnace of affliction was at its hottest. Stephen was martyred as a result of the hostility directed at God's people. If you keep reading Acts, James is eventually martyred as well. As I survey the carnage of Acts 8, I would automatically expect that the church would dwindle and die as they had second thoughts about what they signed up for when they joined the body of Christ. After all, imagine seeing Stephen lying in a pool of blood, dead from the trauma he experienced as they stoned him for a sermon he preached.

That is not exactly a modern-day model of success and church growth. In light of all the challenges, you never read where the church raised the white flag as if to say, "That's enough for me." But reading on, we discover that the adversity produced the opposite effect it was intended to have. Their misery made them multiply. Their pain was productive. While Saul was dragging people out of their homes and incarcerating them, the church continued to advance the cause of Jesus Christ, sinners continued to get saved, and an increase of supernatural power was poured out on the church.

If you look at the Bible carefully, you will see this theme recurring throughout its pages, in the Old Testament and the New. Enemies and attacks were not to be discerned as signs of the absence of the favor of God. The threats and schemes of the adversary were not invitations to retreat. They simply revealed a nervous enemy.

Take Exodus chapter 1, for example. The people of God had been living in Egypt for about four hundred years, having originally gone there to escape famine. While Joseph was in leadership there, Israel lived in favor. Eventually Joseph died and a new Pharaoh arose who did not know Joseph. This meant that Israel had lost its favor. The new Egyptian leader decided that Israel was too mighty and too vast in number to ignore. He chose to oppress the Israelites with harder workloads, more demands, and greater affliction in an effort to reduce their overwhelming strength. However, Exodus 1:12 reveals a flaw in his strategy, an unintended outcome of the increased opposition and oppression. "But the more they [the Egyptians] afflicted them, the more they [the children of Israel] multiplied and grew. And they were in dread of the children of Israel."

Listen to those words. Doesn't that sound almost too good to be true? The enemy does everything he can to hinder, oppose, and limit us, and instead of the hurdle stopping us, it actually becomes a catalyst for growth and multiplication. I believe those who remain submitted to God will cause the devil to regret that he ever messed with them in the first place. The Israelites went into Egypt as a family but came out a nation. Although the Pharaoh wanted to drive them into extinction, his plan to destroy them only caused them to multiply. This is the story of God's people.

PLANTING SEED DURING FAMINE

In Genesis 26 a famine is in the land in which Isaac, Abraham's son, dwells. The Lord tells him not to go to Egypt to escape the famine. God promised to bless Isaac as long as he stayed in the land that God had promised to him and his father.

So Isaac stayed, and he did something no one else did during the time of famine. While everyone else was hedging their risk, Isaac sowed seeds when famine was king. This reinforces an important point. You and I cannot run from the appointed place that God has sent us just because of a famine. God will bless you and the land to which He has called you. Or more applicably, God will bless you and your career and your family. God will bless you in your marriage and in your ministry.

What if famine was not an indicator that you needed to move or give up on the promise God had made you? What if instead it was an indication that you are going to receive a miracle? Isaac refused to leave the land of his father. Rather than waiting for the famine to pass and taking his cues from his environment, Isaac decided to end the famine by breaking the cycle. Isaac planted seed during the famine. Who makes that kind of decision? It seems so frivolous and wasteful to be sowing precious seed in the middle of a drought. Although this action defied logic, it can be explained by understanding the faith Isaac had in the blessing of God. Not only did he reap a harvest in the same year, but he experienced a hundredfold increase in his field.

In Genesis 26:13 the King James Version says that Isaac "went forward." Did you hear that? Isaac went forward in a famine. He advanced in the face of adversity. Grab it, people of God. We have to learn how to operate and thrive even in hostile environments.

OUR FAMINE MIRACLE

God gave this revelation to me in 2008. Our church was exploding in numerical growth, and the leaders and I sensed that God wanted us to enlarge our sanctuary and prepare for future growth. We procured a general contractor and prepared plans to build. But in the middle of our growth and expansion program, the economy of the United States went through the greatest downward spiral since the Great Depression. The housing bubble popped, and a chain reaction of financial woes was unleashed on our country. In the middle of that environment, I was attempting to borrow money to build our church.

I am not sure if you have ever tried to borrow $2.5 million

as a rather new church in the middle of the worst economy in a generation, but I quickly discovered how difficult the prospect of enlarging our church would be. I will never forget the feeling I had after three bankers told me that they could not lend us the money. I was dejected. I felt like a failure as a leader. Even more importantly, I felt as if our people had hit a dead end in our journey. I just did not understand. The crowds were overflowing. We maintained a strong financial balance sheet. All the facts were in our favor. Yet what typically would have been a slam dunk loan process turned into a dire situation for our church family.

It hit me that we were not going to be able to build, so we would not be able to accommodate our growth. Although I was discouraged by the news from the previous three institutions, I decided to have the final meeting with a bank that had yet to visit our campus. I will never forget when Richard Burnette walked into my office at church.

The first thing he said to me was, "I feel God in this church." Now, you need to know that Richard Burnette is a Baptist deacon. I did not know that Baptist deacons could feel anything. (I'm joking.) When he intimated that he sensed God's presence in our little church, I knew we had stepped into the favor of God. Miraculously, six weeks later we had the loan to proceed with our expansion.

You may assume this was the miracle, but it was just the beginning of the forward progress we made during a famine. As we were building our new facility, we planned a stewardship campaign to help us pay off the new loan. But the Lord dealt with my heart, indicating that we could not raise money only to pay off debt on those new buildings. God led us to build an orphanage in Guatemala and a church-planting institute in Uruguay as well.

Much like planting seeds in a famine, building up other ministries and purchasing properties on mission fields while attempting to pay off our own property did not seem very logical. We combined the debt of our new building with the costs of purchasing the property we needed in Uruguay and building of an orphanage in Guatemala. In all, our prayer was to raise 3.9 million dollars for all these projects.

Two significant things happened in the process of launching this financial campaign. First, my youngest son, Isaiah, decided to donate all of the gifts he was given for his ninth birthday. It was a rather large sum of money for a nine-year-old boy.

On the day we launched that campaign, our whole church marched to the altar to give the best offering each family could give God. Guess who was at the front of the line? That's right, Isaiah. As he walked to the front to give his offering, he had a huge smile on his face. Isaiah took over five hundred dollars to the altar and gave it to the building of an orphanage in Guatemala. It was the most sacrificial thing I have ever seen a nine-year-old boy do. I was reminded as I watched him sow that precious seed of what the prophet Isaiah said, "A little child shall lead them" (Isa. 11:6, MEV).

Over the next several weeks, Isaiah would periodically walk up to me and attempt to encourage me with this declaration. "Dad," he would begin his mantra, "God is about to give our church a million dollars." He had no clue the stress mounting in my mind as we approached the beginning of making our principal and interest payment on the new building. Each time he repeated this to me, I became both frustrated and encouraged. I was encouraged that my little son would have the faith to believe for that. Yet I was frustrated that I did not have quite the same level of expectation that he had in his heart.

About the fourth time he mentioned it to me, I asked the Lord how my son could have that much faith while I seemed to have so little. God spoke to my heart and said, "Kevin, Isaiah believes that a significant harvest is coming because he put everything he has into the ground as a seed." You see, when he gave all his birthday money as a gift toward that orphanage, his heart became full of expectation that God was going to honor his generosity.

The second significant moment occurred during a deacon meeting in which we were all suggesting strategies to help us reduce the debt once we began making the payments. I will never forget opening my mouth and saying among all those leaders, "I don't want to give our money to a bank. I want to send it to churches and pastors around the world. And we need to believe God for that harvest."

As soon as those words left my mouth, Dean Sikes, a Spirit-filled deacon in the Lord's church, clapped his hands and prophetically declared, "That harvest will be attached to our seed of obedience." With that, we immediately asked God where He wanted us to give. That night, miraculously and unanimously, our leadership team voted to sow the largest and most sacrificial gift our church had ever given into two inner-city ministries in Chattanooga that were doing the gospel work of feeding the hungry, caring for the orphans and needy, and leading people to Jesus.

The next morning I delivered the checks to the pastors of those churches. They were shocked that we would bless another church in the city. They were overwhelmed at the amount, and I was overwhelmed that we had given it. I could never have been prepared for what God was about to do for our church.

Deven and I had a lunch appointment the very next day with a man and his wife. Mind you, it was a Monday, and you take your life into your hands if you mess with me on Monday. For pastors, Mondays are for recovery. My brain is mushy, my body is tired, and typically my sanctification runs thin on Mondays. Yet for some reason I had agreed to meet this couple on a Monday.

My wife, Deven, wanted to know why they arranged to meet with us, and I did not have a clue. I thought to myself, "If this man has called a meeting to address my sermon or complain about something, I will throw this sweet tea all over him." To this day I cannot remember what I was thinking when I agreed to this lunch together. To be honest, I was still sick from the amount of money we had decided to give away in the deacon's meeting the night before. I was stressed that the principal and interest payments were about to begin on the loan. We needed every dime we could get, and we just gave away more than we had ever given. What in the world were we thinking?

Deven and I reluctantly headed to a local restaurant where we waited for whoever these people were to arrive and introduce themselves. Soon a man wearing flip-flops and a T-shirt walked up with a distinguished lady who was holding an iPad. The hostess notified us that our table was ready for lunch. We sat down with them, and after the initial handshakes and exchanges of greetings, the gentleman looked at me and said, "We would love to hear your story."

Our story? Deven and I looked at each other. We weren't sure how we could cram nine years in the trenches into a one-hour lunch meeting over Kung Pao chicken and fried rice, but we began to share chapters of our journey. After forty-five minutes of describing the details of our ministry adventure, the man looked at me and asked a question I will never forget. "Pastor, can you tell me your debts and your dreams?" Without hesitation I began. I knew both by heart. If you are a young preacher, I admonish you to always carry the amount of debt and the cost of your dreams in your heart. You never know what God is going to do to finance your vision.

I noticed that every time Deven and I mentioned a debt or a dream amount, the dear lady entered that value onto her iPad. After we had explained about the debt for our new church, the cost of the orphanage, the expenses of our church-planting institute in Uruguay, and the cost for our small inner-city campus renovation that we needed to finish, the woman totaled the amount and revealed the bottom line to her husband. He looked at the iPad screen, nodded, and began telling us a revelation God had shared with him during a recent devotional time.

"Pastor," he explained, "I was reading Luke 6:38 where it said, 'Give, and it will be given to you: good measure, pressed down, shaken together, and running over will be put into your bosom.'" His eyes filled with tears as he continued, "I stopped asking God to be the man who received. I asked God to let me be the man who is able to put it back into other men's hands."

With that, he looked at Deven and me and said, "Tomorrow we are going to wire $4.2 million into your account. We are going to pay off your debts and finance your dreams so that you can continue to do what God has called you to do." For once in my life, I was speechless. I spoke in English. I spoke in Spanish. I spoke in tongues. I began to cry. Deven let out a victory shout in the restaurant that almost led to our arrest.

Suddenly, it did not matter how low the market had crashed. It did not matter what other banks thought about our financial strength and stability. In the year of famine, God caused us to experience His supernatural blessing and favor. We did not wait for the famine to end before we followed God in generosity, and God did not wait for the famine to end before He released His harvest of blessing into our lives.

After we had lunch, we immediately left the restaurant to take care of some business. I went to Isaiah's school and picked him up early that day. He bopped down the hallway with his carefree spirit, unaware of the miraculous news I was about to tell him. We quickly headed to the car. After he bounced into the back seat, we departed, ready to share the news. I still had tears in my eyes from my lunch appointment.

I looked into the rearview mirror and saw the most unassuming, childlike face. "Isaiah," I started. "Do you remember when you told me that God was about to give our church a million dollars?"

"Yes, Dad," he replied innocently.

"Well, today God didn't give us a million dollars." A puzzled look came on his face. "He gave us $4.2 million."

I expected him to scream and fall out in the presence of God. Without hesitation he looked at me in the mirror and simply responded, "I told you, Dad."

Wait. That's it? We just had the miracle of a lifetime, and your response is, "I told you, Dad"? There is something simple about childlike faith. I will always remember this lesson my son taught me about faith.

MOVE FORWARD DURING PERILOUS TIMES

In the New Testament we encounter many texts putting us on notice regarding the attack of the enemy. The two letters to Timothy and the letter to Titus are pastoral epistles, all three of which were written by the apostle Paul to his spiritual sons. After Paul successfully planted congregations, he left for his next assignments and placed Timothy and Titus in pastoral leadership over two of these new churches.

Understanding the challenges and difficulties of being a pastor and advancing the kingdom in hostile environments, Paul wrote these three letters to strengthen, exhort, and give instruction to his spiritual sons as they led their congregations. In all three letters, he not only gave them wisdom about how to pastor their churches, but he also encouraged them in their own journeys.

No matter how gifted we are, how successful we are, how victorious we are in one season of life, we need to be encouraged. Timothy and Titus needed to be strengthened. They needed to be reminded that while they would often be faced with adversity and met with opposition, kingdom power would be at work in their hearts that would keep them advancing even in adversity. Today I am thankful that Paul's encouragement to these young men has become the Spirit's encouragement to us to keep on advancing the kingdom and finishing the assignments on our lives even in the midst of adversity.

Adversity will come. There will be challenging, difficult, dangerous times. Paul takes a moment in his second letter to Timothy to articulate the kind of times that would come in Timothy's day and in the last days.

> Know this: In the last days perilous times will come. Men will be lovers of themselves, lovers of money, boastful, proud, blasphemers, disobedient to parents, unthankful, unholy, without natural affection, trucebreakers, slanderers, unrestrained, fierce, despisers of those who are good, traitors, reckless, conceited, lovers of pleasures more than lovers of God, having a form of godliness, but denying its power. Turn away from such people.
>
> —2 TIMOTHY 3:1–5, MEV

This version says "perilous times" will come. The Common English Bible says "dangerous times." The Passion Translation says "fierce" times. This word in the Greek is *chalepos*. It is used only one other time in the New Testament, and that is in Matthew 8 when Jesus comes to the two men full of demons who are living in tombs.[1] The Bible calls these men "extremely fierce" (*chalepos*), so dangerous that they prevented people from passing that way (Matt. 8:28, MEV).

No one wanted to go through that dangerous, fierce, perilous place where two men full of devils were loose. But Jesus took His disciples right into the conflict zone and delivered the men who were bound.

That is the kind of environment that Paul told Timothy would come in the last days: dangerous, perilous, and fierce. Why would perilous times come? The next verse begins with the conjunction "for," which is used to indicate a reason or a cause. Times would become fierce and perilous because of the evil and wicked behavior of humanity (2 Tim. 3:2–5). I want to state this unequivocally: men are not evil because times are perilous. Times are fierce because men are evil. Our godless, self-centered, hedonistic behavior produces a fierce and antagonistic environment for the people of God. This is why at times we feel vexed and grieved.

As Paul continues to dissect the activity surrounding these perilous and fierce times that we are living in, he leaves no confusion.

> But they [those who stand against the truth of God] will not advance, for everyone will see their madness, just as they did with Jannes and Jambres!...But the evil men and sorcerers will progress from bad to worse, deceived and deceiving, as they lead people further from the truth. Yet you must continue to advance in strength with the truth wrapped around your heart, being assured by God that he's the One who has truly taught you all these things.
>
> —2 Timothy 3:9,13–14, TPT

Do you see that progression? Times will become perilous and fierce because godless men will oppose the truth and resist God. In fact, he said they would go from bad to worse. What is his exhortation to young pastor Timothy in light of all this adversity? "You must continue to advance in strength with the truth" (v. 14). No whining. No moaning. No complaining. Darkness will grow darker. You just keep being the light and living in the truth.

That is precisely what God is saying to our generation. It is what He says to everyone who is encountering resistance, attack, and opposition. Keep advancing the gospel. Keep advancing the truth. Instead of continually complaining about the actions of a godless society, be the light. I am afraid we spend more time talking about when they took prayer out of schools than we do starting prayer meetings. What if we used as much energy and resources to adopt a child or fix the foster care problem as we did marching and picketing against abortion? Please do not misunderstand me; I am pro-life to the core. But agents and ambassadors of the kingdom of God are not gifted to simply identify the problem; we are called to bring solutions and be the light.

SAY YES TO GOD

As we have learned in our journey through Acts 8, the church advanced the gospel in the most antagonistic environment imaginable. As I told you earlier, the church was not scattered haplessly. Persecution had caused a sowing of gospel seeds all over the region.

Consider Philip, who was under pressure but still

advancing. He had experienced persecution and scattering but remained under assignment. His "yes" to God was more of a priority than any stipulations or requests. And because of his pursuit of God when life was not exactly comfortable, he reaped a massive harvest.

Philip was initially scattered into a city in Samaria. The Spirit of God worked through the life of this deacon-turned-evangelist to bring revival and awakening to this region steeped in religious tradition. His life is a reminder that titles are not as important as mantles. He was appointed as a deacon in Acts chapter 6. Now he is preaching and demonstrating the power of the kingdom of God as he travels the roads of Samaria. Miracles break out. Lives are changed, and his itinerant ministry results in "great joy" in the city (Acts 8:8).

As revival was breaking out in Samaria, the Lord redirected the evangelist to a remote desert location between Jerusalem and Gaza. A precious Ethiopian brother was reading the Book of Isaiah in his chariot, and God sent Philip to him.

Please do not miss the message in this. Philip had experienced persecution and had fled Jerusalem. Just when he began to experience a measure of revival in Samaria, God assigned him to a desert road with an unconverted Ethiopian brother who did not know Jesus. Yet Philip was not concerned with the size of the crowd, the honorarium, or the numbers the crusade would yield. He left the masses and the multitude for the one.

Let me pause and remind you that every assignment from God that you say yes to is like a stone thrown into a pond. You may think your assignment is about the stone and the pond. But in reality, it is about the ripples that the stone will release. Your yes to God, even in the smallest assignment, will cause a kingdom chain reaction that you will never be able to understand or appreciate until you get to heaven. How do I know this? Because although the Bible shows us the willingness of Philip to accept this seemingly small and uncelebrated assignment, church history reveals the ripples that this one moment of obedience released for an entire people group. For it was through Philip's yes in ministering to this Ethiopian that the gospel would make its way into Ethiopia and other parts of Africa. What if Philip had quit on the gospel when the heat of adversity was being felt throughout Jerusalem? Imagine what he would have missed had he bailed out on the assignment God had given him to reach the Ethiopian eunuch on his way home from Jerusalem. History could have been written very differently.

I feel assigned to encourage you that you will advance even in the face of adversity. God does not need you to wait for your enemy to disappear or the flames to be quenched before you decide to function in your purpose or be used in your calling.

I know we all want the thrill of breakthrough. But there is no time to waste while we wait for our victories to come—and they will come. You will break through into an overflow of the blessings and favor of God. But while you are wrestling the fear in the middle of your storm, in the heat of the fire, decide that you are going to move the kingdom forward. Your most effective moments may not come in a season of tranquility and serenity. God will work through your brokenness and feelings of defeat in a powerful way. If you will decide to give God every trial and every challenging season, He will increase in you.

Paul reminds us in 2 Corinthians 12:9, "My grace is sufficient for you, for My strength is made perfect in weakness." You may not feel like picking up the ball and moving it forward. But you must. Though you may not feel victorious, He is.

Keep putting one foot in front of the other because breakthrough is coming—*after this*.

CHAPTER 5

After This

SO FAR ON this adventure, we have seen the early church experience threats, persecution, plots of opposition and terror, and martyrdom. If you did not know better, you may expect to arrive at this part of the journey and see defeated believers ready to throw in the towel and turn their backs on God.

But the Bible reveals that instead of ongoing anguish and persistent setback, the church was about to come into a new season.

> After this, the church all over Judea, Galilee, and Samaria experienced a season of peace...with the believers being empowered and encouraged.
>
> —ACTS 9:31, TPT

It is hard to imagine that everything could shift on two words, but it did. The life and ministry of the early church made a drastic turn in Acts 9:31 that was described by the two-word phrase "after this" (TPT). The church's miraculous transition was described in such a simple yet decisive way. No marketing program was needed. No sermon series was required. No fanfare was necessary. The end to a pattern of challenges, setbacks, and ongoing warfare was pictured in a short phrase, and a new season ensued. "After this!"

Whatever your *this* is or your *this* was, there is an *after* coming. *After* reminds us that *this* will not be able to hang around forever. A breakthrough is on the way. Job would tell you this is true. The disciples would testify to it as well. Do not make a lifelong sentence out of a temporary season. All the battle, all the warfare, all the fear, all the fighting vanishes when you step into *after this*. God does not have to stay up late and work overtime to help you through the season you have found yourself in. He simply decides that your warfare has ended and your season is going to shift. You have endured the hardship and passed the test, and now it is time for breakthrough in which you reap the harvest.

Perhaps the enemy has done all that he can to create a feeling of hopelessness and defeat in your mind that you just cannot shake. Maybe he has stirred up just enough to distract you from your purpose. It may even seem as if the attacks have piled up against you and your family, and you are wondering when relief will come. *This* can be rough, and Satan wants you to believe that it will last forever.

Do not give up! The early church did not quit or faint in the fight. They are models for demonstrating faith and perseverance. Those who stay in this fight and continue to honor God will inherit a blessing and a breakthrough. In fact, I want to tell you that you are about to be glad that you did not give up! Remember what Paul told the church in Galatians 6:9, "Let us not become weary in doing good, for at the proper time we will reap a harvest if we do not give up" (NIV). The right time will come for those who do not give up.

Hell did everything it could to drive the church out of business in the Book of Acts, but nothing worked. Satan's distraction and his plans of attack will not work against you either. You may look back at something from your past and feel that you barely survived. But right now you are moving on from just a survival mentality. Your victory is imminent. The breakthrough is here. A fresh anointing is coming on your life.

JESUS' BREAKTHROUGH ANOINTING

Seasons changed even in the life of Jesus. In Luke 4 we read that after Jesus' baptism, He went into the wilderness at the leading of the Spirit. For forty days and nights, Satan questioned His deity, attacked His identity as the Son of God, and did all he could to lure Christ into committing sin. Satan's questions to Jesus began with what I call a "satanic if," but each time Jesus responded with a declaration of the Word of God. Our Lord teaches us that when we are under an attack, our strength and victory lie in our ability to stand firmly on the word of the Lord and never give up.

After Jesus firmly resisted the devil, Luke 4:13 says, "And when the devil had ended all the temptation, he departed from him for a season" (KJV). Did you catch that? Satan recognized that he could not defeat Christ in that moment, so he left Him for a season. Imagine the shift that occurred when Satan packed his bags and left the wilderness as a defeated foe. The key to defeating Satan is not in how well we can *rebuke* him but in how well we can *resist* him. James the apostle said, "Resist the devil, and he will flee from you" (Jas. 4:7, MEV).

After having successfully resisted the temptation of the devil, Jesus exited the wilderness in the power of the Spirit, returned to Galilee, and entered a synagogue (Luke 4:14). Upon entering this place of worship in His hometown of Nazareth, He encountered a man who was possessed by a demonic spirit.

Do you believe that Jesus had been in His hometown synagogue before this encounter mentioned in Luke 4? I do. It seems inconceivable that Jesus would not have been there during His childhood or adolescence. I believe both the man and Jesus had been in the synagogue prior to this encounter, but the power of God was not present in Jesus to heal yet.

When Jesus came out of the season of tempting, having overcome Satan in the obscurity of the wilderness, He increased in authority and anointing. He had His breakthrough and was functioning in what I would call His *after this* season. Jesus was led into the wilderness in the Spirit

(Luke 4:1) and He came out of the wilderness in the power of God (Luke 4:14). The pressing and the crushing He experienced in the wilderness produced a fresh anointing in the life of Christ. This was demonstrated when He delivered the man from the bondage of the devil.

When you increase in the power of God, the enemy becomes nervous because of the presence and power of God resting on your life. I do not think anyone who had ever ministered in that synagogue had the kind of anointing resting on them that Jesus had the day He walked into the Nazareth synagogue. That is why a breakthrough came for the demon-possessed man.

AN OLD-FASHIONED BREAKTHROUGH

An *after this* season will come when you experience a breakthrough from God. Breakthrough is not talked about much in the church anymore. Our preference today is for uneventful spiritual experiences that can be managed and monitored without all the collateral excitement that makes people bound by religious tradition squirm. But I still believe in breakthrough. I still believe in the power of God being demonstrated until every bound part of you is set free, everything hindering you is defeated, and everything that was stolen from you has been returned. No bondage. No residue of enemy oppression. Conclusive and total victory will come because of the intervention of God in your life.

I remember that during my battle with COVID, the doctor told me that some patients were struggling to breathe long after the virus had left their bodies. I read article after article and heard report after report of ongoing issues people were experiencing with their lungs. A specialist told me that people were having respiratory difficulties resulting from COVID pneumonia, and they could not even find a cure for this.

To be transparent with you, I felt fear rise up in my heart a number of times. Something as simple as walking to the mailbox often caused an oxygen drop that made me feel dizzy and winded. I wondered if I would be able to preach as I had in the past. I had missed a church conference. I was missing day after day of my children's lives. I tried to push myself into recovery, yet I found myself exhausted from the most menial tasks.

After my quarantine was over and weeks before my doctor gave my lungs the green light, I decided to go back to church to be with the people of God in worship. I came for a few services before I garnered the courage to test my strength and attempt to preach.

I will never forget the first Sunday I was back in the pulpit. My Redemption to the Nations church family had prayed. I had felt the Lord touch my physical body. But the enemy tried to harass me for several weeks with worry and fear because I could not fully regain my strength. Would I be one of the people who dealt with "COVID lungs" for months after the sickness had done its damage? Hearing the doctor tell me that it could be eight to ten weeks before they knew the full scope of any damage did not help my worries subside either.

I made up my mind to take it very easy the week I jumped back into the preaching vein. I paid attention to my breathing as I taught, making sure I did not get too excited in my delivery. I was concerned that my lungs were not going to function properly and that my oxygen would drop if I began to exert too much energy in the delivery of my message.

As I eased my way into the text, I could feel my stamina increasing. I sensed the Lord's presence strengthen me in the middle of my sermon. Yet at the same time, fears bombarded my mind. "You can't do this. You are going to pass out in front of all these people. You will never preach with the strength you once had." I know it sounds impossible, but while I was preaching the truth, I was fighting lies.

As an added safety measure, I had put an oximeter in my pocket when I went into the pulpit. As I sensed the anointing rising in my spirit and felt the power of God moving, I pulled that oximeter out in the middle of my sermon, slid it on my finger, and tested my oxygen. I looked at the reading and broke out into a high praise when I saw the oxygen level was near 100. What happened in that moment is what I call breakthrough. A wave of the power of God shot through me and my church. From that day forward, I have not worried, feared, or slowed down for a minute.

God is the Lord of the breakthrough. "Breakthrough" may seem like a super churchy word reserved only for the spiritually elite or the excited charismatic. But you need the Lord of the breakthrough to go to work for you when your life seems stuck in a season or pattern that is not the life Christ intended for you to live. Jesus Christ can break you through every season of warfare or battle that will ever come in your life.

BORN AGAIN FOR BREAKTHROUGH

I want to encourage you with several facts that ought to give you a backbone of steel, courage for tomorrow, and strength for the journey. First, know that you were born again for breakthrough. You heard me right. When you were born the first time, it was a natural birth. Your earthly mother met your earthly father, and their united DNA along with God's breath of life made you. You have your mother and father's physical features because you were created from them.

But those of you who trust Christ as Savior were not born just once but twice. At the moment you were born again, you took on the attributes of your heavenly Father and began a journey of being formed into the image of Christ. You have the spiritual DNA of the God who knows no defeat.

Some time ago, I wanted to trace my ancestral roots and find out what I could about my background through a DNA test. I wanted to know where I came from. I discovered that a portion of my DNA composition confirmed what I already knew, that I had Welsh, Scottish, and Irish in my blood. Another part of my makeup included DNA from the Congo in Africa. As I thought about the conglomeration of places and people that led to my birth, I was reminded that as much as Satan tries to tear us apart and divide us by our differences in philosophy, skin color, and opinion, the reality of it is that we all really are one big family. If we were able to trace our roots back to their actual origin, we would find that we have common ancestry and common family. In fact, we all came from the first family and our first parents, Adam and Eve. Satan tries to divide us, but we have much more in common than the enemy wants us to realize. We are all members of Adam's family.

As I thought about our spiritual and earthly lineage, I was reminded of an old sitcom we watched as a child. This may date me, but do you remember *The Addams Family?* This television show was about a spooky and dysfunctional family who often behaved in comically weird ways that defied social intelligence. We laughed at them and mocked them, but in reality, they are like all of us. You may feel as if Uncle Fester or Cousin Itt would never be a part of your bloodline, but an honest self-evaluation might reveal that some of their idiosyncratic abnormalities are common to all of us.

The fact that we are part of *Adam's* family explains a lot about the dysfunction, frustration, and cycles of failure we sometimes find ourselves in. We were born into the sin of Adam's family and consequently the pain of Adam's family.

When God created Adam in the garden, He set the stage for him to thrive and succeed. A woman was given to him to be a helpmate, and God talked with Adam face-to-face in the cool of the day. But we are all painfully aware of the fall that ensued in the paradise of God. Tragically, the sin that infected Adam was transmitted to all of humanity. Paul explained it like this in Romans 5:12: "Therefore as sin came into the world through one man and death through sin, so death has spread to all men, because all have sinned" (MEV). Later in Genesis we read that "the Lord saw that the wickedness of man was great in the earth, and that every intent of the thoughts of his heart was only evil continually." God was grieved at what man had devolved into. The curse of sin had spread like a cancer until everyone was obsessed with evil.

What did God do with His defeated creation? He visited a man named Noah to tell him to build an ark because rain was coming and the waters were going to rise. In Genesis chapters 6 through 8 we read about how God in His righteous judgment sent a flood as a drastic measure of His displeasure, saving only Noah, his family, and the animals in the ark. Forty days and forty nights of watery judgment cleansed the earth. Yet when the waters receded, soon after Noah exited the ark, the residue of Adam's sin revved back up and the cycle of defeat and failure started all over again. Time marched on, and humanity continued its destructive plunge.

But when we flip the page from the last Old Testament book of Malachi to the first New Testament book, Matthew, we notice that God pulls out a new play and turns sinful creation on its ear. Instead of scrubbing the earth of humanity's sin as He did in the days of Noah, God decided to start a new race who would not be defined by failure, struggle, and tragedy. Instead, they would be a new creation who experienced the transformational power of grace extended through the person and work of Jesus Christ.

This race of people would exude the power of God as they are born again by His Spirit and come into union with Him. The potency of sin released through Adam's fall was devastating, but the power of grace manifested through the person and work of Christ was even greater. It is precisely why Paul says in 2 Corinthians 5:17, "Therefore, if anyone is in Christ, the new creation has come: The old has gone, the new is here!" (NIV). Peter goes on to describe this fresh spiritual DNA in 1 Peter 2:9: "But you are a chosen generation, a royal priesthood, a holy nation, His own special people, that you may proclaim the praises of Him who called you out of darkness into His marvelous light."

What the first Adam ruined, the last Adam, Jesus Christ, came to restore. When you were born again by His Spirit, you were literally born for victory. Snap out of the thought pattern that leaves you feeling like a victim. You may say, "Pastor, I can't seem to shake myself free from the mental battle that constantly rages in my mind. I don't see an end to the season of *this* I have been walking through." Be encouraged! Those feelings may seem like reality, but they are not the truth. You have been born again by the Holy Spirit. Jesus is not just the champion over sin and Satan; He is the champion of your battle as well. You have the spiritual DNA of breakthrough in you because Christ within you is the Lord of the breakthrough.

MANY BREAKTHROUGHS

The second thing you need to know is that the Lord of the breakthrough is also the Lord of the breakthroughs. Let me explain. In the Old Testament is a story that seems as if it belongs in an episode of *The Jerry Springer Show* more than it does in the holy Word of God. The backstory involves an Old Testament law that provides for the preservation of an Israelite's family, name, and land if he died without children. His widow would be married to his brother to carry on the line in the deceased man's name. It was a righteous thing to carry on the family name in this way in those days.

We read in Genesis 38 that the widow named Tamar was supposed to carry on her late husband's line through his brother. There is more to the story, but eventually, her father-in-law denied her right to do this through his youngest son. So Tamar posed as a prostitute at the gate of the city to lure her father-in-law, Judah (you read that correctly), into an illicit sexual encounter that would leave her pregnant with twins, whom she later named Zerah and Perez. When the day came for the twins to be born, Zerah's hand appeared first. But instead of Zerah making his way out of the womb and inheriting the birthright of the firstborn, Perez came out first and became the firstborn of Tamar and Judah. When his mother looked at him, she exclaimed, "'How did you break through? This breach be upon you!' Therefore his name was called Perez" (Gen. 38:29). Perez meant "breach,"[1] and that name became synonymous with the idea of breakthrough.

You can follow the concept of breakthrough and the power of the name of Perez all the way to the Book of Ruth. The love story of Boaz and Ruth culminates in the last chapter when they receive the blessings of the community leaders at the gate of the city. In Ruth 4:12, elders declare over the couple, "May your house be like the house of Perez, whom Tamar bore to Judah, because of the offspring which the Lord will give you from this young woman."

Many years after Perez attained his own personal breakthrough, his descendants would be blessed with the grace and anointing of breakthroughs for their own homes. Perez began what I call the "house of breakthroughs." While he fought for his initial breakthrough, history reveals that he also began a series of breakthroughs for his bloodline.

The breakthrough Perez began lasted for generations. What began in Genesis 38 with the breakthrough of Perez was perpetuated in his lineage to Boaz and Ruth. But the breakthrough extended beyond them to their son, Obed. He later had a son named Jesse, who had a son named David. Yes, King David came through that house and line of breakthrough.

You may have to fight for your breakthrough! But when you see the breakthrough come, know that you are breaking through for many in your family who will come behind you.

Although David was from the house of breakthrough, he needed to receive a personal revelation of breakthrough. You can come from the house of breakthrough but still be in need of your own personal revelation of breakthrough. David could not simply live off the breakthrough of those who came before him in his family tree. Why not? Because the enemy is stubborn; he tests the freedom and authority of each generation. That is why every generation needs voices who are declaring the message of breakthrough. Every family needs a voice of breakthrough. That is why you cannot give up in the middle of whatever you are going through. You are not only fighting for your breakthrough, but you are also contending for the breakthrough of your family.

After Saul passed away and David occupied the throne, the enemy arrived to try the grit and spirit of the new king. The Philistines had laid low for a while, but now they elected to test the king of Israel. The anointing on David attracted an enemy.

You are not being attacked because you are *flawed*; you are attacked because you are *favored* by God. The enemy does not waste his time attacking you if you are not carrying anything that makes him nervous. But when you have something in you that makes hell tremble, namely the presence of the person of Jesus Christ, he will come against you because of who you carry. If you are under attack today, if you have been fighting something, if you have been walking through tough times, if you have been dealing with adversaries, it is not because you are not favored by God. It is because the anointing of God and favor on your life has attracted an adversary. However, if the anointing on you *attracts* an enemy, it will also *take care* of your enemy. God will never put on you more than you can bear. No weapon formed against you will be able to prosper (Isa. 54:17).

After seeking the Lord, David went to the valley of Rephaim to overtake the Philistines. *Rapha* means "giant" in Hebrew. By adding the masculine Hebrew suffix *'im* to the singular word, it becomes plural. Literally, this is the valley of giants. David finds himself in a familiar place dealing with a familiar enemy. The giants have come back because he is under the anointing.

When David arrives there, he asks God if he should go up against them and God says yes. Before you get in a fight, I encourage you to ask God how to fight. He will give you a strategy that will guarantee your success. When you have heard the voice of the Lord tell you that you are going to win, you can walk onto the battlefield and say, "God's got this."

Religious tradition tells us that insecurity and humility are one and the same. Some approach the battlefield as if being unsure of God's promises is a sign of true spiritual maturity. The reality is that God wants you to trust not in your own ability but in His Word. This is not picking a fight in arrogance but accepting an assignment from the Lord to defeat this enemy. If we continue to walk in His will and honor His Word, Yahweh will give us victory in every situation.

God delivers the Philistines into David's hand, and he utterly defeats them. David renames the valley where the battle took place because of the victory God gave him there. It had historically been a valley of giants, but David renamed it Baal Perazim (2 Sam. 5:20). Remember Perez? His name and his blessing showed up in Ruth 4 as a mantle of favor laid on the lives of Boaz and Ruth on their wedding day. Here in 2 Samuel 5, his distant grandson, David, has invoked the blessing of Perez in a valley after a tremendous victory. Perez broke through, and now David broke through too.

But David does something that I find significant. He adds an *'im* to Perez, which makes it plural. God is the Lord of the breakthrough, and we use this text to preach that message. But in the Hebrew language, God is the Lord of the breakthrough*s*. Do not miss this! He is not just the

Lord of one breakthrough in a life filled with many enemies. You and I need more than one breakthrough. We need the Lord of the *breakthroughs*! Why do you need breakthroughs? Because you may have more than one bad season. You may have more than one encounter with sickness. You may have more than one battle with the enemy over your children, your marriage, and your family.

This is not a semantic "nothingburger." I believe it is a prophetic declaration of your victory in every situation. God will show up time and time again and continually break you through every line of Satan's attack. Although David defeated the Philistines in 2 Samuel 5, Scripture teaches us that the Philistines came back again. God gave David a new battle strategy in the second fight, but the outcome was the same: David utterly defeated the Philistines. Remember: *the enemy is never going to quit, but he is always going to lose.*

Every time the enemy shows up, another breakthrough is yours for the taking! I love the fact that David named the place of his victory after the Lord's breakthroughs. This reminded him, Israel, and even his enemy that the valley was where the Lord of the breakthrough had broken through for them on multiple occasions. Never get used to the battle; get used to the breakthrough in the battle. God has not run out of breakthroughs for you, and he has not run out of breakthroughs for you family.

What do we do after COVID-19? What do we do after a devastating divorce? How do we respond to the attacks that come against our bodies or minds? We do not quit. We believe that as citizens of the kingdom of God, we are promised a measure of joy. The church has to come out of a cave mentality and a posture of defeat and a spirit of heaviness. Do not get used to the heat in the fire. You will not be staying there much longer. I believe one of the enemy's great assignments is to rob the church of her faith and expectation for breakthrough. We have taught coping skills rather than how to conquer, so we have to recapture our faith for breakthrough.

I want to remind you that weeping, sorrow, and pain have an expiration date. Do not believe the storm is going to last forever.

There is an *after this* in the next chapter of your life. In it, the first thing you will need to do is get your vision back.

CHAPTER 6

Check Your Vision

WHEN I WAS thirteen, Saturday mornings were reserved for indulging in my secret habit. It was not a cigarette out behind the house or rolling dice with friends down the block. My hush-hush activity was watching cartoons. My family was well aware of my weekly vice, but early-teen me would have been mortified had everyone else known that I still spent weekend mornings watching *The Real Ghostbusters, ThunderCats,* and the *Teenage Mutant Ninja Turtles.* Looking back, I realize all my peers were at home doing the same thing.

One Saturday morning, all was well in our home. I was eating cereal and watching cartoons when my mother received an unexpected call notifying her that an emergency at the manufacturing plant where she worked meant she was needed immediately. Normally that would have been fine, but my father, an avid fisherman to this day, had departed before daylight for a fishing tournament. Mom had no choice but to leave us. In a slight panic, she gathered her things and assured my younger sister and me that she would return quickly.

"Keep the door locked," she said. Following a few more motherly instructions regarding breakfast and chore delegation, she loaded her things and was on her way.

"I got this, Mom," I encouraged her as she disappeared through the door.

It was a beautiful fall morning. My parents were out of the house, which kind of made me the man in charge of the kingdom for the next few hours. This was the life. It was time for some serious cartoon watching.

My television sat on a chest of drawers at the foot of my bed. I lay on my back, looking at the television between my feet, as the characters I idolized battled heroically against a motley lineup of nefarious foes. My sister lay in the twin bed on the opposite the side of the room from my bed. The sounds of explosions, sirens, karate-fueled fights, and those witty superhero one-liners filled the air. After about thirty minutes, or one episode and fifteen really cool commercials, we heard a thundering noise that was not coming from the TV.

"What was that?" one of us asked.

"I don't know."

More loud banging.

"You go check."

"No, you go check."

The racket was so loud that it shook the house. I lay there aware that my solemn role as the interim man of the house meant I had to do something. But I was quite unsure what that something was. Finally, I rallied my courage and rose from my bed. I slipped as quietly as I could to the front door, sliding along in my sock feet. A few ninja moves later, I was looking through the peephole. I tried to get a glimpse of the crazed maniac who, by the sound of it, had been attempting to tear our house apart, board by board. The reconnaissance mission came up empty because by the time I arrived at the front door, the noise and the perpetrator responsible for it had vanished. Just to be sure, I looked through the peephole again and reassured myself no one was there.

Suddenly, a series of loud booms thundered through the house. Without delay, I sprinted toward the source of the sound. Somebody was about to get the full measure of my cartoon-trained martial arts ability. I was in full-on hero mode now, or at least I was until I caught sight of something that made my blood run cold.

The mystery of the banging was solved, but it was the stuff of nightmares. There against the Saturday sun was the silhouette of a giant man filling the frame of the sliding glass door. I froze as the hulking intruder with murderous intent continued beating violently on the glass door. Even though the thin curtain was enough to stop him from seeing us, I knew that once he got in, he would find us, and we would be dead meat.

"O God, don't let him break it." My prayer was barely audible above the pounding. Miraculously, the door held.

Not to be dissuaded, the burglar switched to a new tactic, pulling on the frame of the glass. He pulled until I thought the door would come off its track. Thankfully, the door was not only locked but surprisingly sturdy. The criminal continued his attempted invasion while I stood there speechless.

My thoughts raced as I tried formulating a plan. I had nothing. Finally, I convinced my feet to move. I quickly ran back to my room and grabbed a phone.

"Call 911," I commanded as I tossed the phone to my sister.

"What are you going to do?" she asked.

"I'm going to hide!" The hero stuff was great for the cartoons, but not when the bad guy was actually on your back porch.

We dove into my closet. My sister was too frozen to make the call, so I dialed 911. The seconds seemed like an eternity as we waited for someone to answer. Meanwhile, I could still hear the relentless attempts at forced entry by this lawbreaker, who I imagined had a felony sheet as long as a Tennessee highway. What was he going to do when he got in here?

"What is your emergency?" The voice of the 911 operator brought me back to the moment.

I whispered desperately, "A man is breaking into my house, and he is trying to kill me and my sister."

She urged me to remain calm and quiet and not leave our hiding place until the police arrived. We waited in that dark closet for what seemed like a year. She stayed on the phone with us, and soon I could hear what sounded like hundreds of sirens approaching from every corner of the city. They grew closer until I heard tires screeching on the streets around our home. I felt a glimmer of hope because deliverance from this vile ruffian was imminent. The operator assured me that the house was surrounded and the police would protect our lives. A few minutes later, I heard muffled shouts as the police yelled out commands to the villain. We were saved!

"Young man," said the operator, "the SWAT team has apprehended the suspect." Relief flooded my soul. She then proceeded to inform me that they wanted us at the front door. My sister and I were overjoyed. We would live to see another day!

As we approached the door, we heard something confusing. Although the SWAT team had captured the suspect, he was loudly and with great animation maintaining his innocence. Even though their guns were drawn and pointed in his direction, the man, who sounded strangely familiar to me, pleaded for the officers to believe his explanation.

"I am their father," the lunatic was exclaiming. "This is my house!"

I opened the front door, and my relief turned to despair. Standing there handcuffed and surrounded by thirty policemen was my father with a look on his face that I had seen just one or two other times in my life. I had only barely survived both those encounters.

At that point, I began to contemplate my mortality. Graduation from middle school was suddenly questionable. Marriage and children were probably not going to happen. I was toast. Today was my day to die after all.

I cannot remember much about the next few days. Psychologists say we block out painful chapters of our lives. Nonetheless, I am still here, but by the grace of God.

What lesson do I want to share with you from that true story? Perception is your reality! What you see and how you see are critical to both your decision making and your expectations.

Had I just looked behind the curtain of that sliding glass door, I would have recognized that big shadow of a brute to be my loving father who left his fishing tournament early when he found out his kids were home alone. He came home to be with us. To my natural eye it looked as if someone was trying to kill us. My fear was founded on a false perception, not reality. Since I was not seeing rightly, my judgments and reactions were terribly flawed.

The same is true in our spiritual journey. We often reduce our hope, limit our expectations, and diminish our dreams because we are not perceiving reality correctly. In other words, we are not seeing spiritually.

CHECK YOUR VISION

Whenever we emerge from a *this* season of life, the first thing we must do is check our vision. Vision is the primary target the enemy attempts to distort in your journey. Why? Because Satan understands that by barraging our eyes with frightening images and filling our ears with fear-inducing voices, he can effectively paralyze believers. Satan wants you to see the threat and lose the vision. You may ask, "What exactly do you mean by vision?" Vision is the ability to see the plan and purpose of God for your future. It is almost as if God gave you a divine commercial of what is to come. It is convincing and persuasive. It causes you to believe for it although you haven't seen it come to pass yet.

Proper vision, along with discerning assessment of what we observe, is critical. Remember, vision is so paramount to our spiritual lives that Scripture says, "Where there is no vision, the people perish" (Prov. 29:18, MEV).

Of all the battles we find ourselves in, the struggle to maintain vision may be the single most significant of our time. It is no secret that we have been operating in a hostile spiritual climate. This antagonistic milieu has a way of altering our vision. Remember, your vision is affected by your environment.

To demonstrate this, let me describe the hills of Tennessee in April when the pollen is so thick it literally changes the color of the air. My nose runs, my voice leaves, and my eyes swell as the powder from a variety of spring plant life floats in the air. I have to wear sunglasses, keep eye drops in stock, and continually wipe the tears from my eyes. Simply put, environment can affect vision.

Many factors can cloud the spiritual environment—a pandemic, a divorce, a church split, or a child who has forsaken God and everything you have taught her. All these have one thing in common: they will be used by the enemy to hinder our vision. Every time you wrestle through a fight of faith, you are combatting an enemy with an agenda to rob you of vision.

In today's environment, we must be doubly cautious about what we allow to enter our eye gates because it will affect our spiritual vision. As you and I watch the unfolding events of a seemingly chaotic world, remember that often things are not what they seem. Many times we see images that present us with a reality that, in fact, is not the reality. Be careful what you allow to shape your vision.

So, why am I taking the time to emphasize the importance of vision? Because vision is not just something that we might want. For those who desire to walk in victory and advance the kingdom of God, vision is not optional. It is a necessity. Spiritual vision stirs that internal belief that God is in your future. It is the divine commercial about the God things that are to come. Without vision, we lose our hope for the future and find ourselves languishing in the present.

VISION VS. SIGHT

We all have two ways of seeing: vision and sight. Vision offers a vastly different outlook than mere natural sight. We see by sight (natural) and we see by vision (spiritual). Which of these you choose and the observations that come from it will determine whether you walk in joy, peace, and victory, or depression, worry, and fear.

Having natural sight is of great importance. Our physical eyes provide us with the ability to see the natural world around us. I am thankful that I can take in the blue sky, the mountains, and the light given by the sun. Nevertheless, to be relegated to living with natural sight and no spiritual vision is to live with the greatest limitation in life. Natural eyes can reveal what God has done, but spiritual eyes allow us to see things that God is going to do. With vision, we catch a glimpse of things by faith, things that extend beyond the current circumstances.

The premiere biblical illustration of the difference

between sight and vision is Bartimaeus, the blind man who taught us something powerful about vision (Mark 10:46–52). While Bartimaeus could not see the material world, he possessed spiritual vision that led to a miracle. To call him lacking in sight would be accurate. But in vision, he surpassed those around him, including Jesus' own disciples.

When Bartimaeus heard Jesus was passing by, his vision, not his sight, propelled him to cry out to Jesus for mercy. This led to a life-changing encounter with Jesus and the restoration of his sight.

Be careful that you do not miss your moment with the King because you have lost your vision. Like Bartimaeus, you may not be able to see it in the natural, but keep your heart full of spiritual vision. Bartimaeus told himself to cry out to Jesus, an act that would have seemed pointless to a person with more sight and less vision. But Bart had an internal conviction that if Jesus would just move in his direction, his life would never be the same again. His miraculous healing revealed that his vision was accurate.

Bartimaeus perfectly illustrates the two kinds of seeing and the importance of having true vision. I plead with you not to accept the inferior form. Your vision must be so powerful that it prevails over the sight of your circumstances. You must stay in a place of vision. Your spiritual tomorrow will never be reached if you cannot see past today.

The enemy's plan to paralyze the people of God succeeds only if we perceive our lives and our journey through the wrong lens. Too many people are making long-term decisions based on temporal situations. They have no vision.

Too many churches are making spiritual decisions based on natural things. They too have lost their vision. Sadly, for churches and individual believers alike, the loss of vision is the first symptom of the loss of destiny.

My prayer is that God intercepts every plan of the enemy to steal our vision. COVID tried to steal it. The enemy tried to purloin it. Life tried to drain it. Religious systems tried to pilfer it. Unfaithful friends tried to embezzle it. *This* moments tried to rob it. Yet even now, I sense God is restoring your ability to see spiritually.

In Psalm 27:13, David said, "I had fainted, unless I had believed to see the goodness of the LORD in the land of the living" (KJV). Fainting, or succumbing to the circumstances, and the lack of vision are connected. Your desire to throw in the towel is directly related to your inability to perceive spiritual vision for your future. You cannot faint now. God is doing so much more than you can see in the natural. You just need the vision to see it. Take a pause and ask God to give you fresh vision right now. In Jesus' name, receive a fresh dose of spiritual vision!

Something fresh is happening on the earth, and God is inviting you to be part of what is next—*after this*. I know that *next* may seem like an unusual concept at a time when you may be trying to just get through the *now*. But *next* is coming. Do not get stuck in what used to be. Instead, get ready for *next*! The children of Israel camped out in the wilderness for a season, but it was not where they were headed. This is not where you are going to stay! Move with the cloud.

THE POWER OF SPIRITUAL VISION

Scripture is full of this concept of vision. The sixth chapter of 2 Kings records the story of a prophet named Elisha and his nameless servant who were facing the army of the king of Aram. This king had continually set up ambushes against Israel, but Israel thwarted every one of them.

Finally, the king of Aram called a meeting of his top strategists and advisers to figure out what was going wrong. He arrived at the only logical conclusion: there must be a snitch in the Aramean army. Things were about to get ugly. An ancient king trying to find a spy is an incredibly dangerous individual. Fortunately for all the potential suspects, someone in the room knew what was really going on.

One of the king's advisers spoke up and said, "Elisha, the prophet who is in Israel, tells the king of Israel the words that you speak in your bedroom" (2 Kings 6:12, MEV). Millenia before the CIA, the private quarters of the king of Aram had been tapped by the Holy Spirit. Every detail of Aram's plans was being revealed to the prophet Elisha. At this revelation, the king of Aram sent an entire army to surround and apprehend one prophet. Imagine that! One prophet with spiritual vision had become such a threat to the enemy that an entire army was dispatched to deal with him.

The Aramean army arrived at Dothan in pursuit of the man of God. Elisha's servant looked out in the morning to see a devastating scene. The city was surrounded by Aramean soldiers with horses and chariots, and they looked serious. The servant rushed back in fearfully and asked Elisha what they were to do.

Notice the generational implications of this text. A young servant runs to a seasoned prophet, a spiritual father, to inform him just how dire the circumstances are. The young servant had probably never felt so horrified. He had never been so outnumbered. This may have been the first time the servant had ever been faced with a "certain death" scenario. This was terrifying!

The servant was probably not expecting the response he got from Elisha. The first thing that the prophet (father) said to the servant (son) was, "Do not fear" (2 Kings 6:16). Fear is how we respond to things we do not know how to handle. These moments are opportunities to demonstrate faith in God, yet when things are outside of our control or understanding, anxiety seems to be our default.

The sentiment in this command to the servant is found in the New Testament when an apostolic father named Paul told his spiritual son Timothy, "God has not given us a spirit of fear, but of power and of love and of a sound mind" (2 Tim. 1:7). As spiritual fathers, both Paul and Elisha understood that fear did not come from God. And if fear does not come from God, you can overcome it.

The prophet Elisha told his fearful servant, "Those who are with us are more than those who are with them" (2 Kings 6:16). If I had been the servant, I would have humbly asked, "Where are those who are with us? Where can I find them?"

The servant and the prophet were proclaiming differing observations because they were seeing through different sets of eyes. To see as the prophet saw, the servant would have to perceive with spiritual eyes. The servant had younger and stronger physical eyes, but Elisha was looking into a realm the servant had never detected. Thus, the servant saw the fierce Aramean army while Elisha saw heavenly allies surrounding them in the form of spiritual horses and chariots of fire.

The servant needed new vision to realize things were not as bad as they looked. If you are looking around and seeing the enemy, if you are noticing all the reasons to give up, if you find yourself not sure if you are going to make it out of your situation, then you are just like the servant. Find a way to tap into your spiritual perception. I do this by reminding myself of what God said.

I find that it is helpful to journal. When God gives a promise or a prophetic word, if we write it in a journal, we can go back to remind ourselves of what God said. Then the journal becomes an aid that helps us keep our perspective in line with His purpose and plan for our lives. God's words to us are like weapons that combat the schemes of our lying adversary. What you see with your natural eyes may look distressing, but reality is not as bad as it seems. Something is already transpiring in the invisible realm. An unseen move of the Holy Spirit is getting ready to take care of what you are worried about in the seen world. Oh, for the vision to see it!

The very nature of God is what places the spiritual visionary at a distinct advantage over an adversary. God has perfect understanding of the future before it ever arrives. So, the person with spiritual vision is operating from a perspective that exists outside of time. This is why, when you walk by Holy Spirit vision, you are always one step ahead of your enemy.

God wants to open your eyes to what He has been doing. You have been worrying, and you have lost sleep. You have been trying to push away the anxiety. But, right now, the Word is declaring, "Those who are with us are more than those who are with them" (2 Kings 6:16).

This is not a dismissal of your trouble or an attempted downsizing of the devils you have been fighting. It is a reminder that, the bigger your enemy, the greater the host of heaven who are fighting with you. I am praying like Elisha, "Lord, open their eyes!"

THE ENEMY IS BLIND

When Elisha prayed, God not only gave the servant vision to see the heavenly army, but he also closed the eyes of the enemy. Did you catch that? God gave vision to the servant and took it away from the Arameans. This reveal how critical having vision is.

Here is the massive advantage you have over your enemy: the devil is blind. No matter how clever you may believe him to be, he cannot see what God is doing. When he plans his attack, he is oblivious to the fact that for every weapon he is raising, God is moving to use it for His glory. If you are struggling to believe that, let me show you a powerful reminder in the Scriptures.

Paul speaks of God's hidden wisdom in Christ's crucifixion resulting in the salvation of the world. In 1 Corinthians 2:8 he writes, "None of the rulers of this age knew; for had they known, they would not have crucified the Lord of glory."

While God was working the plan of redemption, He never allowed Satan to know what was actually happening. When the Roman soldier took the cat-o'-nine-tails and whipped the back of Jesus, blood poured out. In the natural, it looked like the unconscionable treatment of a holy man. In the natural, it was flesh being torn. In the natural, His sides were being shredded. In the natural, blood vessels were exploding. But this was not only a natural event.

Something was happening in the spirit. Cancer was leaving your body, depression was fleeing from your house, your addicted family member was being set free, and your marriage was being restored. In the natural, it was an execution. But in the spiritual, it was the breaking of sin and every generational curse, and the releasing of blessing upon your house. And the devil was blind to the whole thing!

The devil was not just without sight when it came to the crucifixion of Christ. He is also lacking perception when it comes to the persecution of those of us who are in Christ. If the devil knew what God was doing in you, he would have left you alone long ago. If he only knew that everything he throws at you is being used for your good, he would have stopped attacking. But he persists because he is blind.

In the days ahead, as you pray intentionally about your spiritual sight, watch what happens. Not only is God going to open your eyes and give you 20/20 spiritual vision, but He will also smite your enemy with blindness. This next season is going to be a contrast between clarity and confusion. You will be taking steps of progress in clarity, while your enemy stumbles in confusion. It is vital that you are intentional regarding the development and maintenance of your spiritual vision.

RECALIBRATE YOUR VISION

When you come out of a *this* season, you can take some practical steps to regain lost vision. We just talked about Elisha, but his mentor, Elijah, is a great example of vision restoration. In 1 Kings chapter 19, we find Elijah hiding out in a cave. This is a startling turn of events because the man who is secreted away in a cave had just been used by God in one of the greatest spiritual victories ever recorded.

Elijah had been Yahweh's representative in a years-long showdown that pitted the king of Israel, Ahab, against the King of the universe. In a display of God's power, Elijah prayed and drought came. Later he prayed again, and the drought stopped. But before the rains returned, Elijah participated in an epic conflict on Mount Carmel's slopes between the one true God and the prophets of the false god, Baal. Elijah prayed a short prayer, and literal fire fell from heaven. The man of God then slew 450 false prophets of Baal. If ESPN covered spiritual combat, Elijah's highlight reel would make him the spiritual heavyweight champion of the world. He was mightily used by God and looked invincible.

Jezebel, King Ahab's wife, was furious over the killing of her prophets. Baal worship was Jezebel's pet religion, and those priests had been loyal to her. She threatened to kill Elijah, and for some reason, the seemingly invincible prophet was jolted by her menacing threat. The man who had just taken down Baal's battalion was now running for his life. Elijah fled to Horeb, the mountain of God. There, during his *this* moment, the prophet holed up in a cave, his ministry shut down by the words of the wicked queen.

"What are you doing here, Elijah?" the Lord asked him (1 Kings 19:9).

The voice of God broke into Elijah's shameful situation. God is so gracious (and not just to Old Testament prophets) that He did not show up and scold Elijah. He just asked him a question—one that helped Elijah open his spiritual eyes and see exactly where he was and just how he got there. Sometimes God does not send us a sermon, a lecture, or even a lengthy conversation. Instead, He just pricks our heart with the question, "What are you doing here?" In those moments, He is prompting us to use our spiritual eyes.

After patiently hearing Elijah's fatalistic justification of his newfound timidity, God told the prophet to step out onto the mountain. As Elijah stood outside the cave, he experienced a strong wind, an earthquake, and fire. Surely, he would find God in all those manifestations. Yet remarkably, the text says that God was not in any of them. Then came a soft whisper.

When Elijah heard that, he took his mantle off and put it around his head and went outside the cave. What a strange thing to do. Why would he engage in such an inane action in this revelatory moment? I believe this was the recalibration of the prophet's spiritual hearing and spiritual vision. He knew he could no longer be driven by what he was perceiving with his natural senses. He needed his spiritual sight restored. He needed vision reestablished. It was as if God revealed to Elijah that naturalistic thinking had stolen his courage and stalled his advance. God wanted the prophet to see beyond the natural odds and hear a different voice than the one threatening him. God was teaching Elijah something we all need to remember: you cannot fight spiritual battles based on natural observations.

Thankfully, Elijah recognized his vision deficit. When he wrapped his head in his mantle, it was as if he were saying, "I can't be led by my natural eyes and hear only by my natural ears. I need to see with spiritual sight and be recalibrated to the voice of God again."

There comes a time in every battle and every moment of overwhelming anxiety in which you and I must follow Elijah's lead. We must assess whether we have been forming our thoughts, and ultimately our actions, based on what we are observing in the natural or on what we see with our spiritual eyes. If we find that our thinking and our doing are not in alignment with what the Word has taught us, then it is time to wrap our heads in our mantles and recalibrate.

Recalibration of vision may mean different things for different people, and it may even vary depending on the season or the situation. We have settled for getting our vision from the culture or from the media. Some of you may need to stop watching the news. For others, it may be time for a social media fast. You may limit your availability to friends or family members who walk in negativity and toxicity. Whatever it takes to make sure you are walking by spiritual sight, do it. Spiritual blindness is not an option.

Today, may a tribe of Spirit-led people arise, wrap their heads in their mantles, and choose to walk by the Spirit again. May we have ears to hear and spiritual eyes to see what God is saying and doing in our day.

Natural sight is not enough. After *this* you must recalibrate your spiritual vision. Then you can move forward in God's strength.

CHAPTER 7

From Strength to Strength

WHEN GOD GIVES you a breakthrough and changes the season you are in, He elevates you into greater dimensions of His strength. In the time of *after this,* your eyes are opened and your vision is refined because you passed the test. You overcame and persevered. Just as God brought the early church out of an intense season of warfare and into a season of strength, He will soon bring you into a new strength that comes from Him. I prophetically declare that you are stepping into fresh strength that you have not known.

> Then the churches throughout all Judea and Galilee and Samaria had peace and were built up. And walking in the fear of the Lord and in the comfort of the Holy Spirit, they were multiplied.
>
> —ACTS 9:31, MEV

In this scripture, God describes believers who are in this new season of strength. The Greek word *oikodomeō* used here is translated "edify" in some Bible versions and "strengthen" in others. It carries the idea of building something solidly.[1]

When I think about a season of increased strength like this, I think immediately of Psalm 84. Charles Spurgeon called Psalm 84 the pearl of the psalms.[2] It is a powerful song of worship, written by Korah, compiled by David. In it, the psalmist reveals his pursuit of the presence of the Lord.

Here the psalmist finds himself yearning for the opportunity to be in the house of God. He intensely longs to dwell in the courts of the Lord and in His presence. Reading this psalm, you can hear the craving in the heart of the psalmist. Nothing other than God will satisfy his heart. For those who hunger for God, no cheap religious imitation will suffice! Nothing in this world will ever compare to the presence of the Lord. Nothing else will quench the thirst of those who thirst after the living God. The hunger you have for Him will bring you into the strength of this new season.

PURSUING GOD

Any Jewish man reading this psalm would recognize that hunger and thirst for God is demonstrated in more than just empty words. There is an active pursuit occurring. Those truly hungry for God seek Him. In Psalm 84:5 the psalmist speaks of those who have set their heart on a *pilgrimage*. When a Jewish man or a Jewish family heard that word, they knew that the psalmist was talking about the set times in the year when feasts would take place in Israel.

At those times, Jewish families would pack up and head to Jerusalem to honor and worship their faithful God. This represents the pilgrimage of pursuit, of going after God. If we are hungry for God, we will pursue His presence. We will make the investment necessary to go after the person of God and pursue Him in prayer, fasting, and the Word.

Paul spent his entire life trying to chase down the One who had chased him down. If God has ever chased you down and touched your heart with His love, your proper response is to spend the rest of your life longing for and pursuing Him. This involves more than a visit on Sunday. My soul longs to be in the presence of the Lord all the time. Because of this hunger, the psalmist says we launch out on a pilgrimage in pursuit of God.

In 2 Corinthians 3:18, Paul declares that we move from glory to glory. We do not just sit down in one level of glory, and we do not just park ourselves where we have always been. We take a journey that leads us from glory to glory, from faith to faith. We do not stay as we have been; we grow into everything God has called us to be until we get into His presence.

We are on this journey to the glory of God, from one dimension of God to the next dimension, from one depth of God to the next. There is more of God! He is not just the God of yesterday; He is the God of today and He is the God of what is still to come. There is more of Him that you and I have ever known or witnessed.

The psalmist says in Psalm 84:10, "I would rather be a doorkeeper in the house of my God than dwell in the tents of the wicked" (NIV). Do you understand what that means? It means I do not need a title, a special seat, or accolades from others. I would just rather go to church and prop the door open so people can get into the house than dwell in the tents of wicked people who do not know God.

When the psalmist says he would rather be a doorkeeper, I immediately think back to a story about the ark of the covenant and a man named Obed-Edom. King David, after establishing his new administration in Jerusalem, decided to bring the ark back to Jerusalem. In 1 Chronicles 13 we read that David utilized a cart to carry the ark, which worked well for a while. But everything came to a screeching halt when David, his entourage, and the ark of the covenant arrived at Nachon's threshing floor. The oxen pulling the cart stumbled, and Uzzah put out his hand to steady the ark. Immediately he was struck by God and fell dead. Many scholars believe Uzzah had gotten common with holy things and lost his sense of reverence for God.

Despite the goodness of God, this incident caused fear, and rightly so. Uzzah was dead. No doubt discussions broke out about what to do with the ark and how they should handle it going forward. I am sure David and the leaders searched the holy law to determine where the breach occurred and how to prevent that from happening again. But until they knew what to do, the question remained, "Where will we park this ark?"

The Scriptures don't give us the details, but I imagine it was at this point that a man named Obed-Edom stepped forward. He was more convinced that God is good than that He is harsh. In my mind's eye, I can see him lifting his hand and saying, "You can park the ark at my house!" Do you feel that way? Let the mighty argue it out. "You guys can have the deep debates and heavy theological conversations," I can picture Obed-Edom saying. "While you parse the details, please know you can park the ark at my house. I am hungry for the presence of God."

For ninety days, the ark of the covenant found a resting place in Obed-Edom's house. The Bible tells us the Lord blessed Obed-Edom and everything that belonged to him on account of the ark (1 Chron. 13:13–14; 2 Sam. 6:11–13). Some traditional Jewish rabbinical writings go so far as to say God blessed Obed-Edom's wife and eight daughters-in-law to have children each of the three months the ark was in his house.[3]

David saw the favor of God resting on the house of Obed-Edom and decided to bring the ark back to Jerusalem. When David went to get the ark, it seems as if Obed-Edom and his entire family decided that they would rather move with the ark than live without God's presence. It is possible that they might have packed up their house and gone with David and the ark to its new place. Why might we think that? In 1 Chronicles 15, Obed-Edom is listed as a doorkeeper in the temple. Perhaps they moved to Jerusalem because they did not want to live without the glory of the Lord. The incredible news is that if you and I will hunger for Him and make space to host Him, God will come to our houses and release His favor on our lives.

PASSING THROUGH THE VALLEYS

As we continue this journey in Psalm 84, I must tell you that this path of pilgrimage goes through the Valley of Bacca (v. 6). In Hebrew, this means the valley of "weeping." Jewish pilgrims would load up their families, pack up their children, and march toward their ancestral homeland with the desire to stand in the presence of God and honor Him in their worship. Yet on that journey was an inescapable trail that led through a valley.

We often avoid trails like these in our journeys because we are unable to understand why people who love God go through challenges, vicissitudes, trials, and tribulations—and, dare I say, the valley of weeping. We talk a lot about joy, but remember that joy comes after a certain season. It does not matter how holy you are, how many tongues you speak in, how many mission trips you have been on, how many gifts you operate in, or how much you love God. If you are on a pilgrimage to see His face, you will walk through valleys, through seasons of *this*.

David went to a valley called Rephaim on his way to fight the Philistines. Hosea mentioned the Valley of Achor, which means "trouble" or "causing sorrow" (Hos. 2:15).[4] Joshua also had a sorrowful experience in the Valley of Achor (Josh. 7:24–26). David wrote about the valley of the shadow of death (Ps. 23:4). Jesus passed through the Kidron Valley on His way to Gethsemane (John 18:1). Valleys, dark seasons, and seasons of weeping are not just for the defeated or hurting. Even the godliest who are hungry for the Lord experience them.

You will walk through valleys in your life. In some seasons you will have faith one moment and have to fight off fear the next. You will see yourself surrounded by dark mountains that impose themselves upon you. While you are walking through a valley on your way to see God, your tears will flow. Personally, I have tried to rebuke the valley, but to no avail. I have tried to bind the valley, but without success. No matter what confession I made, I had to walk through the valley and endure the moment of *this.*

Some of you say, "I love God; I am on the Lord's side. Yet I have some stuff going on in my life, some troubles in my mind, some sorrow in my heart. I am torn, and I feel as if my life is out of control. If people could peel back my exterior and really see what was going on, they would see that I feel crazy. Do I have it together? Am I going in the right direction?" But the psalmist reveals that you are headed in the right direction if you find yourself walking through a valley of tears.

I get nervous about people who never have to walk through a valley. Valleys taught me tenderness and how to sit with those who are hurting. Valleys taught me how to have compassion on those victimized by the assassins of life. Valleys showed me how to have compassion for people who feel broken on their journey.

The sweet news is that when you come to a valley, you do not stay there. The Bible says that we *pass through* (Ps. 84:6). It does not say you get stuck in it! You do not come to the valley to die in it. Whenever you come to a valley, recognize that this is not going to last forever. Pick up your pace a little bit. Remember, you are just *passing through* this valley! You are passing through this depression, this pain, weeping, and sorrow. You are not going to stay there. You are coming out to an *after this*.

As the psalmist continues to describe this journey, he reveals a profound truth about those who are in a valley yet pursuing the presence of God. He says, "They make it a place of springs" (Ps. 84:6). I would think this should say, "God gave them a spring," but it says that they made it a spring. You and I have to learn how to make lemonade out of lemons.

In the valley, you need to love people, show kindness, and serve others. You have to discover how to make a spring in the middle of your valley. You have to learn to say, "It is not happening for me right now. Doors aren't opening, but I refuse to be selfish and not open a door for someone else." You must decide that you will have a spring in your valley. You can be walking through a valley and still be a blessing to other people. You do not have to wait to get out of your valley to demonstrate the goodness of God to other people. Make it a spring! Make the valley wish it had never messed with you. Run the devil completely out of your life by being just like Jesus in the middle of your valley. The valley cannot keep you from creating springs in your life. Decide that the heavier the sorrow or pressure, the sweeter will be the spring coming out of your life. Do not wait until the valley ends to make it a spring.

The psalmist then tells us that "the autumn rains also cover it with pools" (Ps. 84:6, NIV). The word translated "pools" means blessing.[5] Just when it seemed that the parched, weary sojourner could not take another step, an empty hole filled with the rain of blessing and created a refreshing pool in the middle of the scorching heat. I prophesy that seasons are going to change in your valley. Showers of blessing will come. Can you imagine while traveling to the temple, you pass through the valley and make it a spring? The rain comes. The pools that were dry start filling up and overflowing. You actually do not have to be out of the valley before God blesses you. God will bless you while you are in your valley. There will be showers of blessings. Dry seasons are over!

FROM STRENGTH TO STRENGTH

The promise that came to the pilgrim psalmist also came to the early church in Acts 9, and it is going to come to you as well: "They go from strength to strength" (Ps. 84:7). There is not a route to God that does not have a valley. However, remember that as you go through valleys, something is happening that you cannot feel or see. You are not simply moving from valley to valley. In reality, you are moving from strength to strength. You are getting stronger, and you do not even know it. The enemy thought you would get weaker, but God says you are getting stronger. You may think you cannot make it, that you should just go back home. But another voice in your heart tells you to keep on walking. What you are walking into is better than what you walked away from. If you keep on walking, if you stay in the *pursuit*, what you will walk into will make you forget about the pain. That is why the psalmist said, "Better is one day in your courts than a thousand elsewhere" (Ps. 84:10, NIV).

In this psalm, the word "strength" is used three times. In the first usage, "strength" ('ōz) means might or power.[6] The second and third time the word "strength" is used, the writer uses the Hebrew word *chayil*, which describes might or even brute force. *Chayil* (also spelled *hayil*) has a unique and deep meaning that includes the idea of courage or valor in addition to physical strength.[7]

Chayil shows up in Judges 6:12 when the angel of the Lord calls Gideon a "mighty man of valor" (*chayil*). Gideon was hiding from the marauding Midianites, but God called him a mighty man. God saw a man who was hiding and told him he had valor. Perhaps you feel more like Gideon than a man or woman of great valor. God sees you as mighty. God will call you what you will not call yourself!

When Gideon discovered God had guaranteed him victory, he decided to fight. Gideon was led by God to gather only a small band of men to defeat the vast camp of Midianites. God also gave them an unusual battle plan that did not involve any battle, but it did produce a supernatural victory over the Midianites. In the same way, God will soon shift you out of a place of hiding into the place of victory, and He is not going to use conventional means to do it.

WONDER WOMEN

The word *chayil* is used in Proverbs 31:10 when describing a "virtuous woman." The word translated "virtuous" is *chayil*. A virtuous woman knows how to bake with one hand and bind the enemy with the other. Sisters, you know how to change diapers with one hand and lay the other hand on your ailing baby, saying, "You shall live and not die." God is raising up women who not only know how to balance a checkbook but also know how to open up the windows of heaven in the marketplace where the kingdom of God has never been experienced before.

Ladies, I encourage you to be virtuous. That doesn't mean be perfect and performance driven. It means that you will not give in to the culture that is assaulting the minds of your children and attacking the core of your home. You are a woman of *chayil*. As you rise up in the strength of God, know that you have the grace to make the enemy wish he never attacked you or your family. Be strong. Be courageous.

Solomon asked, "Who can find a woman with *chayil*? The earth is looking for these kind of godly women, and I see them rising up in our generation. Saying this is not slighting the brothers. I have no desire to confuse roles or create competition between the sexes. But women who operate in valor and strength are needed in this moment of history.

If you have ever seen the 2017 movie *Wonder Woman*, you know exactly what I am talking about. It is set during the First World War. A segment of land existed between the Central Powers and the Allied powers, which was known as No Man's Land. History reveals that this land was a death trap for any man to cross. In the movie, no one from either side was courageous enough to cross it.

Upon seeing the evil, the terror, and the carnage that the Central Powers were exacting against innocent people, Wonder Woman looks at her beau and informs him, "We cannot leave without helping them. These people are dying."

"This is No Man's Land, Diana. It means no man can cross it," he replies.

Rather than arguing, she recognizes that although no man could cross this land, she could, for she was no man. She runs across this war-torn battlefield, ultimately leading the Allied Forces into a victory in this scene. With all due respect to the brothers and the God-given role they have, some battles in our generation are being fought by *chayil* women.

I am a big teddy bear. I am a lover not a fighter. I can get torqued up if I have to, but by and large I am a maker of peace. But Deven, my wife? Not so much. A few years ago on vacation we had a day at the pool with our family. My four kids and their cousins were throwing a squishy ball soaked with water in the pool. My son Isaiah and his cousin got a little excited and carelessly threw the ball over in an area of the pool where a woman was sunbathing on her float. The ball never hit her. I repeat, it never touched her. What it did do was send a splash of water onto her feet and the float.

The woman, who surely had a bad day—or more likely, a horrible year—decided she would express her frustration with Generation Y by taking it all out on my son. She grabbed his ball and began to taunt him. She threatened to destroy the ball. She threatened his person.

I just stood there without the wherewithal to help my son survive the onslaught of madness coming from this lady. Just as I started to wonder if my son would live to graduate from high school, my wife descended from the tanning deck, dove into the pool, and, like a crocodile preparing to prey on an innocent baby animal, waded to the area where the woman was. I saw *chayil* rise up in my wife. I saw the look in her eyes.

I immediately went from worrying about my son and his future to worrying about the poor lady who had incited the bear. "Dear lady," I thought, "don't poke the bear!" You can mess with a number of things and Deven will not pay any attention. But mess with her children, her family, or her church, and you provoke another part of her that could end world wars. Deven unpolitely reached into the woman's space and, without asking with her normal congeniality, snatched the ball from the woman.

Dumbfounded, I went under the water partly embarrassed that I had not intervened and partly humiliated that the entire resort saw my wife go off on the dear lady. Had TikTok been a thing at the time, my wife would have become a viral sensation.

It is *chayil* courage and tenacity that women in our day need as they intercept the attacks of the enemy! I believe women of God will lead the battle for life in the womb and to the tomb. I believe our sisters with *chayil* strength supplied by God will lead movements and organizations that will help end human trafficking in our day. Woman of God, I pray that the *chayil* strength of Yahweh rise up in you!

THE WEALTH OF GOD

Before he died, Moses gathered the children of Israel together and shared his final words of wisdom. "Remember the Lord thy God: for it is he that giveth thee power to get wealth that he may establish his covenant" (Deut. 8:18, KJV). The Hebrew word that we translate "wealth" is *chayil*. When you are living with the *chayil* strength of God, the wealth of heaven is resting on your life!

Moses was talking to a generation of people whose parents and grandparents had lived as slaves in Egypt. Their ancestors had been there over four hundred years. Many of them probably had a defeated slavery mentality. Yet Moses reminded them that their God was able and willing to give them the ability to experience increase. God essentially empowered ex-slaves to live in the abundant blessings of heaven and have what they needed when they needed it. That is true wealth—access to the provision and blessing of God.

I sincerely believe that kingdom resources are coming into the lives of those who are focused on fulfilling kingdom purposes and who are ready to advance the agenda of the King. You may have been raised in poverty and lack, but if God gave Israel blessings in the Old Covenant under the leadership of Moses, how much more will He bless you who have put your faith in His Son, Jesus.

NEW LEVEL OF POWER

Remember that the journey you take in pursuit of God may lead you into the valley. But your valley is not your tomb. The devil did not give you life and he is not able to take it away. As long as you remain humble, obedient, and yielded to God, you are virtually indestructible until God finishes the masterpiece that He started with your life. If you are walking through a valley and God has not yet fulfilled this word, just keep on walking, keep on dancing, keep on praying, and keep on praising! You are coming through with a new level of strength in your life!

The enemy thought he would kill you in the valley, but the valley became your launching pad. God is getting you through, and you are not coming out the way you came in. Instead, you are coming out in a new anointing, and a new level of blessing and authority. The enemy will wish that he had never messed with you.

All these instances of the use of *chayil* reinforce the truth that God is moving you from strength to strength. You will walk out of *this* valley in a new dimension of the power of God. The Lord will give you power to move from one level of courage to new levels of courage, from one level of virtue to new levels of virtue, and from one level of wealth to new levels of wealth!

You will need God's new level of *chayil* because God has more for you.

CHAPTER 8

The God Who Is to Come

I BELIEVE IN THE more of God, and I want you to believe in that too. When you understand this concept, you will find your faith increased and your assurance deepened. Comprehending this principle is the antidote to status-quo thinking and the catalyst to sustainable momentum. I firmly believe that a church preaching the more of God will be a church who lives in a sustained revival and discipleship cycle. I know it sounds as if I am promising a lot, but the power of appreciating the reality of more cannot be overstated.

Simply put, the more of God is the idea that no matter how good He has been, more of His goodness is still to be revealed. In moments you are faced with seemingly insurmountable obstacles and, conversely, in the moments when it feels as if things could not get any better, God still has more goodness in store. God is going to reveal more of Himself because He is good. No matter how deep you have gone in your journey, no matter how much of Himself God has already revealed to you, there is more.

Prophetically speaking, I believe we are on the verge of the kingdom experiencing the more of God in unprecedented ways. A generation of believers is declaring that no matter what they have face, no matter the condition of the world around them, and no matter the apathy of other believers, they are hungry for God. The beautiful thing about being hungry for God is that He always responds to those who desire Him. If you seek, if you hunger, if you desire more, God will give you what you are seeking.

This is the hour. You are going to experience more of His goodness. The broken are going to find more of His love. Those seeking will find more of His power. Not everyone will experience this promise, but only those who refuse to be satisfied with the status quo.

Expecting more becomes your default setting when you walk in the knowledge that God loves giving new seasons and opening new doors. I know that the concept of new seasons, new doors, and new blessings is easy to criticize. It sounds overly optimistic and even belongs on the list of modern Christian cliches. Yet the very nature of God is one of Creator and giver of new life, which includes new seasons. Furthermore, God consistently calls us into deeper understanding and greater glory. God wants you to experience His "more," to experience more of Him.

I once preached a message called "God Is Not Through Blessing You." I believe that promise is for you. We are so often caught up in what we are going through that every trouble seems final. Sometimes we believe that all we have encountered has brought us to this most recent difficulty, and it is going to be the end of us. This could not be further from the truth. God is not finished; He has more. God is going to bless your life despite the season of pain, loss, and warfare you may be experiencing now.

In some theological circles, it has become popular to attack any preaching that refers to the blessings of God in this life. Sermons regarding the promises of God in relation to temporal things are labeled as "prosperity gospel" and dismissed as "less than" and shallow. Before you dismiss what I am saying, understand that this is not pie-in-the-sky, name-it-and-claim-it Christianity. God's blessing on those who keep the faith and stand strong when faced with life's most challenging moments is a biblical norm with solid scriptural precedent.

NOTHING IS FINAL

Imagine what the disciples felt when their Messiah was hanging on a cross. When the word came that Joseph of Arimathea had taken His lifeless body and placed it in a tomb, it must have felt like the end. They had experienced difficulties before, but this was different. Tombs are not temporary; tombs are final.

We all have had moments in our lives that felt final. Perhaps you had a public failure. Maybe your perfect marriage ended in divorce, or an unexpected loss or setback hit you out of the blue. Sure, some people said encouraging words to you, but they just did not understand what you thought you knew: that this was as final as a tomb.

You found yourself in a place of "no more"—no more hope, no more life, no more vision, no more chances, no more tomorrows, and no more reason to think it was ever going to change. It was final.

But come with me to Sunday because on that day, the same tomb that declared the end declares that God is not through because death became life. Just yesterday, the tomb brought a sense of dread, loss, and utter hopelessness. But on Sunday, there is a strange absence of fear and darkness. Peace takes its place. Jesus is alive! The end becomes the beginning because God is doing *more*.

The resurrection story never gets old. It is the foundation for every ounce of hope we possess. In John 20 we read that Peter was told by Mary Magdalene that Jesus' body was no longer in the tomb. So Peter and John raced to the tomb to see what the commotion was all about. To their shock, the body of Jesus was not to be found because He had risen! This incredible three-year journey was not over as they had thought. There was more to come.

Word began to spread throughout every hamlet and village in Judea. The wonderworking teacher who had been publicly executed was alive, just as He had predicted. Then, if being resurrected was not enough, He hung around for forty days and made Himself known to many. In those six weeks, He appeared to over five hundred witnesses (1 Cor. 15:6). Throughout His time on the earth, Jesus had healed the sick, preached the gospel of the kingdom, and demonstrated the power and authority of God to those who followed Him. As the resurrection story built toward its climax, Jesus led His disciples up a hillside where He gave a final promise before departing earth.

"You shall receive power when the Holy Spirit has come upon you" (Acts 1:8).

Before His followers could even formulate their typical questions, He finished this prophetic farewell message, ascended upward until a cloud received Him, and disappeared from their sight, ascending to the right hand of God the Father (Acts 1:9). Dumbfounded, this group of disciples—the ones who were to be the foundation of the church—stood staring at the sky the way children watch a balloon disappear from sight. Can you imagine the hearts of His disciples as they watched Jesus fade from sight?

We have the benefit of knowing the rest of the story, but for the disciples standing on that Judean knoll that day, watching their Savior leave must have felt like the end. The ascension was certainly not accompanied with the trauma of the cross, but in many ways, it must have felt even more final. But their story was far from over. They soon realized that what seemed to be a climactic end was actually a revolutionary beginning. God was not through. The best was yet to come!

GOD IS NOT FINISHED

Acts chapter 1 is no false start or literary misdirection. From this account forward through the whole Book of Acts, we see an ongoing revealing of the power and the glory of God. Every setting, every situation, every story calls the reader further into understanding that, when it comes to God, there is no end in sight. No matter how miraculous the event we read in Acts, with every turn of the page we see more. The gospel is carried far beyond Jerusalem, people are converted, the Spirit is poured out—and then we read on to find that the kingdom of God advances even more.

"I am not through yet!" may not be found in the Greek manuscripts, but God seems to be shouting it in every verse of Acts. You cannot read the book without coming to the conclusion that, with God, there is always more.

Please do yourself a favor and read Acts as if it were a story. If you are a minister, do not look for a sermon or a teaching topic (those will come), do not just read a couple of verses (although just a few verses are powerful), but simply take it all in. Read it like the biography of the bride of Christ it was intended to be. It is a riveting narrative from beginning to end that never veers from its powerful refrain, "There is more."

You would think that by the end of Acts, we would fully grasp the more concept. Yet there remain some who believe this glorious story of God's work on earth ends in Acts 28 at the conclusion of Luke's writing. Some see Acts 28 as the end of the apostolic era, the conclusion of a season that displayed the might and power of God. This thinking creates a false division between then and now, and thus renders the Book of Acts irrelevant for our day. With such a view, Acts becomes a catalog of history, a story of antiquity, an irrelevant synthesis of early church tales that have no import or consequence on our modern-day church paradigms.

THERE IS MORE OF GOD

But others of us believe that the story of God's redemptive plan and the expansion of God's kingdom on earth is still gloriously unfolding. We believe the Book of Acts is still being written—not in the canonical sense, but in the practical ways God continues to show that He is not through yet. We walk in confidence that the very omnipotence of God, one of His essential characteristics, necessitates that there is more of God's power hidden than has ever been revealed. We believe in the more of God: that there is more of God's glory, more of God's power, more of God's love, more of God's redemption, and more of God's miraculous works to come! We believe there are more healings to experience, more salvations to celebrate, more towns to be turned upside down. I believe in the more of God, and I am inviting you to believe with me!

My faith is the "evidence of things not seen" (Heb. 11:1), but "not seen" does not mean unfounded or groundless. The thought of the more of God flows from a truth that is repeatedly revealed in the Bible: you will never find a time when God is finished. There will never be an end of Him. In fact, I challenge you to find the end of God in Scripture. Find the place where the totality of God is revealed with finality. Show me where man has explored the depths of God's love and found the bottom. Search the Scriptures and inform me where adventuring explorers reached the edge of God's power and declared, "That's it. There is no more."

We can spend a lifetime searching for the end of God

and never find it. He has no beginning, and of Him there is no end. The unfolding of His person and His glory are infinite. Let me show you what Scripture says about this. In Revelation 4, in the heavenly throne room of eternity, John the Revelator gives us a glimpse of an eternal worship service that is continuously occurring in the abode of God.

> The four living creatures had six wings each, and they were covered with eyes all around. All day and night, without ceasing, they were saying: "'Holy, holy, holy, Lord God Almighty, who was, and is, and is to come.'"
>
> —REVELATION 4:8, MEV

In our limited understanding, we cannot begin to fathom the sights and sounds the Revelator describes as he observes worship in the heavenly realm. The scene that John is being pulled into is happening in an eternal context, which is why it feels so otherworldly. The living creatures and the proclamations of holy worthiness are all part of the glorious worship that the apostle has been invited to view. Entire sermons, books, and studies have been written about John's heavenly tour, but what strikes me beyond all of the activity and glory described by John is the declaration being made by the four six-winged creatures. Listen again as he describes these celestial beings worshipping our everlasting God eternally.

Revelation 4:8 says, "The four living creatures, each having six wings, were full of eyes around and within. And they do not rest day or night, saying: 'Holy, holy, holy, Lord God Almighty, *who was and is and is to come*!'" (emphasis added).

The God who was

If we are not careful, we can get so caught up in what we hope God will do that we lose sight of all He has already done. But the testimony of His goodness already realized informs our faith in His goodness yet to be revealed. The worship of God is clearly impossible without honoring Him for all His faithfulness and acknowledging that He has been in control and in charge throughout all of history.

Some say God is hard to find, but anyone who is looking can see this "God who was" operating in His creation from the beginning. His fingerprints can be detected in Abraham's encounter on Mount Moriah and Moses' experience at the Red Sea. God was there in the Valley of Elah when a diminutive shepherd with a homemade sling and a pouch of stones slew a Philistine champion. The "God who was" flattened the walls of Jericho, and that same God shook a Philippian jail until the prison released the two preachers it held. The "God who was" tricked the Moabite army through sunlight reflecting off ditches full of water and brought a victory for His people. Thousands of years later, in 1588, it was the "Protestant wind," sent by that same, faithful God, that confounded the Spanish armada and kept the reforming church from destruction.

Look back and see the "God who was" shaping all of history. His sovereign hand crushed kings and kingdoms, and elevated nations and peoples. By His power, voices emerged that molded generations, leaders were birthed, movements began, militaries were defeated, governments were overthrown, and history was shaped. Again and again, we view His hand moving things toward an ultimate end that redeems His creation and glorifies His name.

Looking back on God's hand in history is enlightening and encouraging, but the "God who was" does not just describes an aloof God superintending the broad and general history of mankind. Scripture reveals that this "God who was" is intimately aware of the smallest details of your life. He was faithful to Abraham, Isaac, and Jacob... and Kevin...and you.

God has been working in both the seen and unseen realms in your life ever since you were born—and even before you arrived here. Just look back at what you have been through. Without the "God who was," you would have gone down a long time ago. His faithful presence in every chapter of your past explains how you survived it. Every time we gather to worship corporately, or even when we adore Him with no one else in the room, may we worship Him for who He has been, all He has done, and the ways we have seen the "God who was" in our lives.

The God who is

The worship of God in Revelation 4 flows out of what God has done and who He has been in our past. But the words of the heavenly creatures also acknowledge Him as the "God who is." He is not simply the God of antiquity and the God who walked with biblical patriarchs and filled the cupboards of church mothers throughout modern church history; He is also the God who is active right now. If I were in my pulpit, we would have to take a praise break right here!

Vital to the health of a robust worship life is the simultaneous awareness that God was and God is. You cannot fully worship Him if you refuse to take inventory of your life and acknowledge the faithfulness of the "God who was." But a knowledge of God that only celebrates Him in the past can still leave you feeling hopeless in your present.

We also need a revelation that in the *now* of our lives, God *is,* and He is worthy to be worshipped. Not only *has* He done, but He *is* doing. I not only see God when I look back; I also find Him as I look around. I choose to acknowledge that He is the "God who is" in the nasty now. We can see Him despite what the media and the puppet-master moguls of public perception try to get us to see. When we look at the X-ray revealing the mass in a loved one's organ, we still see God. When the bills are high and we hear the rumors of layoffs, we still see Him. In the midst of betrayal, heartache, and hardship, God still *is.*

I am so grateful that God is not just the God of then, but He is the God of now. It is this knowledge that shows us that praise is in order no matter what we are dealing with. The enemy operates with an agenda that includes trying to stop us from praising God in the now.

This may come as a surprise to you, but Satan is not terribly disturbed when you worship God for what He has done in the past. It would take a fool to look around and not acknowledge the hand of God. So, Satan is not particularly surprised or even bothered when you acknowledge the reality of God in the past. However, the last thing he wants is for you to start recognizing God's presence in the now and giving Him praise for it.

When you praise the "God who was," you acknowledge history. But when you praise the "God who is," you affirm hope. Satan may spit at your remembrance of what God already did, but he shakes when you start realizing what God is doing in your present situation. Whatever situation you are in, take time to praise the "God who is." Do not be limited to praising God for what He has done. Join the heavenly host and worship the "God who is."

God was a healer; God is a healer. God was a deliverer; God is a deliverer. God was a provider; God is a provider. God was my rescuer; God is my rescuer. God was then. God is now.

He is the God who was. He is the God who is.

The God who is to come

We have seen God in the past, we have acknowledged God in the present, but praise is not complete until we realize that the God who was, and the God who is, is also the God who is to come.

We have a tendency to think that when we see God in eternity, we will have arrived at the culmination of this adventure of knowing God. One look and we will have a full understanding. We will have seen it all, and then we can hang out in heaven for the next few millennia rehearsing the history of God through the testimonies of the family of God. Somehow, I think this concept is selling the experience short.

Consider this. Even in heaven, in the full light of eternity, the six-winged creatures are telling us something about the character, might, splendor, and glory of almighty Yahweh.

The place they exist transcends time and space, yet they are declaring that He is the God who is to come. Did you get that? They are in celestial worship, but they are declaring there is more to come. They are residing in a dimension beyond time and space, a place of perpetual continuity, and yet the six-winged creatures tell us He is to come.

The idea that God is yet to come reveals the necessity of a timeless, unending, infinite procession of existence that we call eternity. Eternity must exist because it is the vehicle designed to reveal the unfolding glory of God. Without eternity, there can be no sufficient unveiling of His glory. Since the greatness of His power and glory are unending, there cannot be an end to eternity. By definition, eternity has no end. Functionally, it is not merely what is, but it is what has yet to be. Without eternity, there would be no vehicle to reveal the glory of God, because His glory has no end.

What is the point? Sure, it is fun to talk about eternity. It is an enjoyable thought exercise, entertaining the existence of an endless progression of moments. It is awe inspiring to recognize that after a million years of revelation, more of His glory will have yet to be revealed. But what does that mean to us?

If heaven cannot hold the totality and fullness of God's glory, then the storm, the season, and the setback you have just come through will not be the end. No matter how much of God has already been revealed in your life, no matter how many prayers He has answered, no matter how often He has been your supply, there is more of Him to come. God was, He is, and still there is more. You may be at the end of you, but you will never come to the end of Him!

The time has come for the church to step into full recognition of the more of God. It is time for you to rip the lid of limitation off your expectations. You know Him. You have seen His power. You have experienced measures of His glory. You have witnessed revival. You have waded in the river of His awakening. But hear me, there is still more of God's glory hidden than has ever been revealed.

It is an insult to God for us to act as if we have seen what there is of Him. From the presence of God in the wilderness tabernacle to the throne room visions of Ezekiel, Isaiah, and John, when God opens a window into the heavenly, He reveals patterns of truth that we ought to be walking in on earth. If heaven, the eternal realized, is declaring there is more of God to come, how much more should we on earth recognize that there is far more of Him to experience here.

Family, there is more. There is more of God to experience at your storefront church. There is more of God for the church you have been pastoring for forty years. There is more of God than they taught in your church planting class. There is more of God after the revival has ended, more of God after the blind lady gets healed, more of God after you write that Grammy-winning song, more of God after you preach that amazing sermon. There is more. In fact, when we get heaven, pick up our robes, put on our crowns, and sing "How Great Thou Art" for the first ten thousand years of eternity, we will discover that we have just begun to behold the beauty of His splendor. He is the God who is to come.

This is why you must believe again. Even while you sit

there in the mess of the mistake you made, there is more. Pastor, when you sit down after another Sunday and wonder if you are just going through the motions until you retire, there is more. Church planter, when your support dries up and the first six families you won decide they are going to follow the couple on your launch team who is starting a new church in their home, there is more. Married person, when you have tried all you know to do and yet your spouse seems further from God than ever, there is more. Parents, when you have prayed every prayer, read every book, and talked to every expert about your troubled child, there is more.

The fact that He is the "God who is to come" causes hope to burst through that dark veil of hopelessness the enemy has tried to drape over our generation. That is precisely why Paul says, "Our light affliction, which lasts but for a moment, works for us a far more exceeding and eternal weight of glory" (2 Cor. 4:17, MEV).

Imagine Paul having demonic powers and principalities working against him, people threatening his life, fears without and within. That sounds horrific, but Paul said that all of that mess was a light affliction. Oh, it was real and it was heavy, but when compared with the weight of glory awaiting him, Paul called his affliction "light." If you think your trial is heavy, wait until you experience the weight of glory that is coming on your life. So, while you are in the middle of the trouble, be confident that God is coming, and He is coming with "more."

As you put this book down and think about the reality that there is more, I want you to know that the more of God is not just for people who are in the middle of difficulty or even those who are muddled by the mundane. The more of God is also for those of you who are in a season of blessing, success, and revival. There is still more.

Your church is growing, but there is more. God is healing, yet there is more. Your finances are blessed, but there is more. You are catching fresh revelation every time you open the Bible, and there is more. The gifts have been operating in your life and in your church, yet there is more. It is time for you to start living in the more.

Yes, you know God. You have seen His power and glory revealed.

Guess what? There is *more*.

God wants to bring awe and wonder—and revival!

CHAPTER 9

Revival!

HAVE YOU EVER slept through a storm? You wake up, look out the windows, and see the evidence of the night's turmoil. Your coworkers ask you if you heard the thunder, but you slept right through it. You may hear on the news that an earthquake occurred near you, but you were completely oblivious. Like sleeping through storms or quakes, sometimes things around us shake and break, but we do not even notice it.

You can be oblivious to many things, but I am sure you will know when a breakthrough has occurred in your life. A shift not only happens in the tangible world around you, but a dynamic move of God's Spirit also occurs in your life. You will see the effects around you and feel them within you. Which comes first may vary, but the presence of both of these confirms that God is doing something. In kingdom work, seeing without feeling may be circumstantial, and feeling without seeing may be emotional, but seeing and feeling is revival.

As I mentioned earlier, a spiritual shift occurred in Acts chapter 9, an *after this.* Sometimes we miss the fact that as the season shifted for the early church, an underlying change in the perceptions and attitudes accompanied their spiritual walk. A new level of supernatural awareness accompanied their religious activities. The community of believers possessed a heightened sensitivity to the things of God. The New King James Version of Acts 9:31 reports that they were "walking in the fear of the Lord."

Have you ever wondered what that means? The answer is multifaceted. Their fear of the Lord did not mean they had a dreadful terror of being in the presence of God. But it did mean that they were always aware of God's presence and they acted in accordance with a desire to perpetuate closeness with Him.

In responding to the question about what living in the fear of the Lord is, I often refer to a statement that I heard a minister make years ago: "Live like there is a dove resting on your shoulder and you never want him to fly away." The close proximity to the presence of God that the early church experienced was something they never wanted to lose. If the presence of the Lord comes to rest on your life, you should take special care not to grieve Him or do anything that would cause Him to depart from your life.

As the early church prioritized God's presence, they found their moments of worship and ministry singularly powerful. Like the early church, you can walk in unique anointing and experience the extraordinary. But to do so, His presence must be your priority. When your life is an open invitation for Him, He will show up. Even today, we can make His presence our priority. Every moment is an open invitation.

OUR BREAKTHROUGH

I am not sharing with you from a place of theoretical understanding or secondhand knowledge. I know what it is to step into a time of awe and wonder and the fear of the Lord. Our moment of breakthrough happened about twelve years into pastoring. Deven and I had already experienced so much of God's grace and kindness on our ministry. Our church had been blessed with such tremendous growth that we began adding new campuses. We knew God was at work, but we had no idea just how much He was planning.

Having outgrown several inner-city campus locations, we were back in the hunt for a new one. Then I got a call asking if I had heard that the former Highland Park Baptist Church campus was for sale. That property had not been on my radar at all. It was one of the most prominent and iconic campuses in the entire city of Chattanooga, former home to the largest Independent Baptist church in the nation. When I heard that this expansive property was on the market, something stirred me that we should at least look at it to see if we could glean any hint that God may want us to have it.

"This building is too big for me," I said as I walked through it on the day of our viewing. It was cool to be looking around, but this was far beyond where we were.

But almost as soon as I got the words out of my mouth, I felt God reply into my heart, "This building is not big enough to hold what I am getting ready to do."

That was God. I felt Him stirring within me. At the same time, He was moving behind the scenes in the tangible world. I will never forget the night God provided the final contribution we needed to purchase that campus without one dollar of debt. It was miraculous, but it always is when God is moving.

After we bought it, we quickly went about renovating the property and preparing for the new launch of our inner-city ministry because we felt we had no time to lose. After four months of renovations, we were ready to launch our new campus. It was all adrenaline and anointing. Life was good.

We had an amazing dedication week of services. But I quickly lost my excitement after the dedication crowd subsided, my pastoral and ministry friends flew back to their megachurches, and we had to begin the challenging process of building the needed ministry structure at our new campus.

While we were overjoyed and absolutely grateful for how God had blessed us, the spiritual warfare in that new facility sometimes grew unbearable. Every Sunday when I went to the pulpit, it literally felt as if a demonic principality were sitting on the media booth defying me and laughing as I preached.

We had experienced such great services before. Our other campus in Ooltewah was thriving. But this new assignment brought a level of warfare we had not experienced before. Threats were made against us. Gang leaders marked their territory on our buildings and property. Services seemed restricted somehow, and the spiritual tension was high. I had not experienced such an attack since I had begun pastoring almost fourteen years earlier but did not know what else to do, so we continued to plow ahead with the vision God had given us: to be a life-giving, multicultural, Spirit-empowered church in the heart of downtown Chattanooga.

It was not getting any easier. At times the church seemed so empty and the atmosphere so dead that I honestly wondered if I had missed God's will by moving into the facility. Little did I know the atmosphere was about to change.

"WATCH THIS!"

On a Sunday morning in January 2014, I was preaching in our new campus when I heard something off to my right. "Watch this!"

Those two words were as close to the audible voice of God as I have ever heard. I was so overcome with the moment, so arrested by the presence of God, that I stopped preaching. I am sure the people were wondering what had happened to me. I was wondering the same thing. Some of my closest team members who knew the fight we had been in may have thought, "That's it. Pastor has finally lost his mind." I had just been preaching to my congregation, and now I stood having a conversation with God right in front of everyone.

"Watch what? What do You want me to watch?" I asked the Lord.

I did not know what God meant or what He was doing in the moment, but I did know that I had heard His voice more clearly than I ever had. Now I was wondering what God was going to do. I imagined that the roof was going to blow off our building or that some significant miraculous interruption would happen in the service, but none of those things happened. However, those two words caused me to believe that God was up to something significant in our church and in our lives. I had no clue what was next on the calendar of God, but we would soon find out, and we would never be the same again.

What God was about to do came in the most unassuming, unexpected package that I could have imagined—a man named Damon Thompson. Damon was a new ministry friend whom we invited to speak at a weekend revival for our college and career department. He had the appearance and the grace of a modern-day John the Baptist—a heavy beard; long, shining hair; and perhaps the keenest ear to hear the voice of the Lord in our generation.

The Friday night service was powerful. Hearts were humbled before the Lord, and the altar was full of sons and daughters crying out to God. It was preparation for the outpouring that was to come on the following evening. Saturday night Damon preached, and something happened. My wife, Deven, picked up a microphone and began to sing Bethel Music's "Tip of My Toes." It was the most innocent worship moment you could imagine. It was not a polished arrangement. It was an unscripted, unedited raw expression of her love to Jesus—from the tip of her toes to the top of her head.

Deven repeated the simple chorus over and over until suddenly the One to whom she was singing walked into the room. At that precise moment, a Saturday night gathering immediately turned into a move of God from which I have never recovered. Knowing something significant was happening and not wanting the dove to depart, I asked Damon to stay over until Sunday and preach the morning service. Of all Sundays, it was Super Bowl Sunday.

The Sunday morning service did not disappoint. It was as if we stepped deeper into the river of God. The outpouring of God's presence during that service forever shaped how we pastor and lead our congregation. The glory of God came so strongly up on me that I could not stand on my feet. It was not ankle deep or waist deep or even neck deep—it was waters to swim in.

Before this encounter some would have called me a control freak. Our services were powerful but timed. God was welcome in our church, but we made Him aware of our expectations. That day changed everything. I could not have stopped it if I had wanted to. I could not even walk to the pulpit to redirect what was happening.

While I lay on the floor, wave after wave of the goodness and glory of God touched my heart. Tears flowed freely. One of the most precious things that happens when you enter a season of the awe and wonder of God is that He restores your tears. A tearless church will have a hard time staying in the river of God.

While I was on the ground receiving from the presence of the Lord, the Lord told me to come back to church that night for an evening service. That was a moment of struggle for me. While I was ready and willing to do whatever was necessary to facilitate the move of God, I remembered the massive Super Bowl party we had planned for that evening.

"But, Lord, no one will come to church tonight because everyone is preparing for the Super Bowl party."

"I will be there if you will be there," the Lord responded.

That day I made a decision to cancel the Super Bowl party and host an unplanned, unscheduled night of revival. In those days we did not have a social media footprint to help us get the word out. I simply invited everyone who was hungry for more of God to join me at six o'clock in the evening for revival. Damon stayed on for the evening service though. I prepared him for only a handful of people to be at that service.

All afternoon long I wondered who would come back for more of this outpouring. When I arrived at 5:30 p.m., people were lined up outside. Cars were parked in the road. The place was jam-packed with hungry people who decided that they did not want to live without the Dove of His presence in their lives. I knew then that I was not the only one who recognized how powerful and unique this moment was.

That evening the power of God came on me again. As I lay on the floor for the second time that day, God spoke to my spirit that He wanted to move for the next ninety days in the hearts of our people. Everyone who would connect to this outpouring of God's Spirit would experience the blessing of God on their home and family. This was a season of awe and wonder.

So for ninety days, we watched in wonder as the power of God broke religious chains and set people free. We saw people from every conceivable background with testimonies about every sin you can imagine get saved, baptized, and filled with the Holy Spirit. Miraculously, we baptized just over eleven hundred people during those three months. One night we baptized so many converts that the baptism pool water looked like muddy water collected from the Tennessee River. That dirty water represented hundreds of souls who were cleansed by the power of the blood of Jesus Christ.

MIRACLES IN THE MARKETPLACE

One of the earmarks of a genuine outpouring of the Holy Spirit is that the church experiences as much or more of the glory of God in the marketplace as it does the church building itself. Some of the most notable miracles that happened during the revival occurred outside the walls of our church. It was common to hear testimonies of lives being changed and souls being saved in restaurants, shopping centers, and sporting events throughout our city. I could not write about this season of awe and wonder without telling you some of the stories that we experienced during those ninety days.

One night we did not leave the building until after midnight because of the ministry at the altar. When I finally sensed the release to leave, I took Damon and several brothers to an all-night diner in Chattanooga so we could fellowship and debrief. As we walked into the dining room, I noticed that no one was there except our group and a young lady sitting alone several tables from us. She had a hat pulled down over her eyes. I watched her wipe the tears from her face as she overheard our conversation about what God had done that night in the service.

As we continued to tell the testimonies from that night, a man entered the restaurant and sat down with the young lady who was weeping. I was aware that God was doing something, but I could not discern what was happening and what, if any, action I needed to take.

Suddenly the young man jumped up from his table, turned toward ours, and exclaimed, "Pastor Kevin, we need a miracle." I did not recognize the young man, but he immediately told us their heartbreaking story.

They had a beautiful family, but adultery and infidelity had threatened to destroy it. In fact, they later told us that meeting together that night was to finalize the divorce agreement and decide on child visitation privileges for each of them. As they talked, a few of us moved closer to their table. We could sense that they were both ravaged by the pain of their sin and were in desperate need of hope.

God had more in store for them that night than divorce. The power of God broke in on us in that diner and worked in their hearts. We encouraged this family and prayed for their healing and restoration. Damon slipped a ring off his finger and gave it to the young lady so she could put it on her husband's finger as a sign of her new covenant with him. At well after midnight, with the restaurant staff peeking out from behind the display cases of cakes and desserts, I led them in a renewal of their vows as God saved their family by doing a miracle in their broken marriage.

Though the list of wonders that God worked during this season of revival would not fit into one chapter of this book, I will give you a few highlights. A number of blind people received their sight. A man who had been given up to die from pancreatic cancer was miraculously healed. To this day, the doctors are befuddled as to what happened to his cancer. If they read this book, now they will know.

After this cancer was healed, the faith level of our church exploded. I carried my children to the car after midnight on several nights while they were still speaking in tongues. Law enforcement officers and security details who patrolled our facilities were overwhelmed by the goodness of God. I watched as one of them was slain in the power of God and received the baptism of the Holy Spirit. Drug addicts were set free. Prodigals came back to their kingdom family in droves. It was such a precious and unique season for Deven and me and our church family. We were walking with awareness of the Dove. A sense of reverential fear and wonder captured the hearts of our people in those ninety days. We were cognizant of God being among us, and we did not want Him to leave.

Moments like this are wonderful, but they are not without their challenges. Let me give a word to those leaders who are hungry for revival and awe to come to your church. Do not try to put today's revival in yesterday's wineskin. Some people were frustrated with me because I transitioned the revival from nightly gatherings into a church that was involved in the community and ministering outside our walls.

We began an aggressive outreach strategy that involved food distribution, clothing closets, community partnerships, and a Thanksgiving and Christmas outreach that brought holiday meals to hundreds of families and Christmas presents to over two thousand children. Some people wanted services to go on every night of the week because that was their definition of revival. The transitions I made even led to some accusing me of quenching the Spirit. But I believed that God wanted our church to translate the outpouring He had sent us into being a church that transformed our city and region.

Revival may not look the same in your house as it did in ours. Do not feel compelled to fit yesterday's mold or even into the pattern that we saw develop here in Chattanooga. God will give you a strategy by which you can experience the fire, tend the fire, and keep the fruit of harvest that God is sending you. You do not have to choose between being a revival church or being a growing church. If you are in revival, your church will grow. The outpouring of the Holy Spirit will always draw in the harvest.

I am never going to tell anyone that I have enjoyed all the difficult *this* moments in our lives. No matter how much you spiritualize your trouble and how much faith you walk in, no one enjoys trouble. Yet I can tell you that after you have gone through seasons of difficulty, the Lord will come close and make His presence real. If you press through the hard seasons, you will find yourself at the breakthrough and experience *after this*.

WALK IN HONOR

When you find yourself in an extraordinary season as we found ourselves in, you will want to sustain that access to God. I have discovered some things will help nurture the atmosphere of revival. One of the earmarks of people who stay in the river and live in the blessing of God is that they walk in an extremely high measure of honor. They honor God first and foremost. They also demonstrate a high level of honor for each other.

If you want to know how honor and dishonor affect the work of Christ and His Spirit in your life, look no further than how those from Jesus' hometown of Nazareth treated Him compared with people from Capernaum. Their perception of God and their honor or dishonor for Him directly impacted who He could be and what He could do in their lives.

Exhibit A is found in Mark 6:1–6. Jesus went to His own hometown of Nazareth and taught in their synagogue. While they could not deny the authority and revelation with which He spoke, they also could not accept that He was more than their earthly brother. Their familiarity with Jesus bred a measure of dishonor that kept them from properly perceiving who He was. The Son of God was standing in their midst, and they were treating Him like just another guy in the family.

Jesus' family and friends may not have thought their actions were dishonorable, but dishonor occurs any time you place less value on an object or person than they are truly worth. In this case, they were not seeing Jesus as the Son of God. Lacking spiritual vision, they could only see Him according to the flesh.

When you fail to perceive God's presence and you fail to see that He is moving, you will treat Him with a level of dishonor. Obviously, some revile and curse His name, walking in overt dishonor that is easily recognizable. But most dishonor in our churches shows up in less noticeable ways.

I have been guilty, not of overtly dishonoring God, but of not properly valuing my precious Lord. At times I have failed to see what He was doing in that moment or through a person. Not until the Holy Spirit convicted me did I recognize that I was operating in a manner that brought dishonor into my relationship with Jesus. The moment I find dishonor, I change my actions or thinking, because dishonor can be costly.

When the people of Nazareth dishonored the Lord in His own city, Mark 6:5 records one of the saddest statements in the Gospels: "Now He could do no mighty work there, except that He laid His hands on a few sick people and healed them."

After taking note of their unbelief, Jesus walked out of Nazareth, the place of dishonor. Scripture never records Him returning there again. What a sad commentary for a people who had such potential and possibility. Perhaps no other group of people were better positioned to receive all that heaven was ready to release than the people of Nazareth. Jesus was born there and He grew up there. It obviously occupied a special place in His heart. But He refused to jeopardize His assignment and the anointing of the Holy Spirit by remaining in a place laden with dishonor.

Dishonor literally repels the presence of the Lord. That is why I maintain that dishonor will ruin a season of awe and wonder. When God begins to move in powerful ways, this sense of honor, of walking in the reverential fear and awe of the Lord, keeps Him close.

Conversely, if you look closely at the city of Capernaum, you will discover that Jesus found honor there. I recognize that as a city, Capernaum missed its opportunity to repent and turn to the Lord. (See Matthew 11:23.) Nonetheless, some people in that community adored the Savior. They honored Him because they knew who He was, and their honor created an atmosphere in which God was willing to work.

An example of honor found in the citizenry of Capernaum is Peter, a fisherman whose home was in this coastal city. I have visited the spot where his home is believed to have been located. There Jesus operated in the miraculous. So, it would be good to see what Peter did that gained him this favor with God.

What kind of person was this fisherman who turned into a formidable disciple? A hothead? Check. Obnoxious? Check. Easily pressured? Check. But when Peter was asked who Jesus was, he did not stumble in his speech or have any doublemindedness in his response. Without hesitation or reservation, Peter replied, "You are the Christ, the Son of the living God" (Matt. 16:16). Peter saw Jesus as more than a carpenter from Nazareth. He recognized that Jesus was the Messiah sent from heaven. Peter walked in honor, and he got to see a season of awe and wonder.

If you need more reasons to understand why Jesus would move His entire ministry base to the fishing village of Capernaum, look no further than the story of the centurion. Matthew chapter 8 details the day the centurion came to Jesus to plead for a miracle in the life of his deathly ill servant. Although Jesus offered to come to the man's house to heal the young man, the centurion quickly dropped the greatest revelation bomb ever dropped in that city. In essence, the man recognized the messianic authority on the life of Jesus.

His reply to Jesus went something like this: "Since You are the Messiah, You don't have to come to my house. You have the authority to speak the word and my servant will be healed." When Jesus heard his sermonette and saw his faith, He sent the centurion home with the promise that he would have what he had believed Christ would do for him.

How did the Capernaum centurion know to come to Jesus for healing? At some point he must have heard reports about all that had been done through Jesus, and he decided to believe. Faith is one way we demonstrate honor. When you believe in Jesus, you are declaring that He is who the Word says He is.

Peter, the centurion, and a slew of other citizens of Capernaum received glorious miracles from Jesus because they properly perceived and valued Him as the Son of God. In fact, some of the most notable miracles that Jesus performed happened in Capernaum and its outlying areas. The quality of honor and faith in that community attracted Him, and He responded to that honor and faith with manifestations of His power.

Practice honor in your personal life. Be quick to acknowledge God and give Him the glory for what He is doing in the earth. Do not join the skeptics and cynics who spend their time murmuring and misjudging things they do not understand. You must be careful never to become like the people of Nazareth, who were so familiar with Jesus that they treated His presence as commonplace. In that atmosphere of dishonor, He could never meet the significant spiritual needs they had. Never rush the presence of God and never fail to recognize when He has made His presence known. Honor Him above schedules, plans, traditions, and systems.

Be a person of honor. One of Satan's greatest assignments is to push you into a place of dishonor. You must recognize and resist his insidious plan. Nothing will ruin a season of awe and wonder faster than a spirit of dishonor.

Honor is like the sustain pedal on a piano. A chord creates a beautiful sound, but the sustain pedal causes the sound to last much longer. Honor turns moments into momentum.

Walking in honor is one of the easiest ways to attract and sustain the blessing of God.

Now, a final word to help you keep moving through *this* into *after this*.

CHAPTER 10

Hell in the Hallway

WHEN YOU PUT this book down for the last time, I pray that you have learned to see the faithfulness of God in every situation you face. God is going to be just as faithful in your future. But before going forward, I want to leave you with one last lesson. This may not be the climactic ending you expected, but it is one of the most significant concepts I have discovered for experiencing the more of God. It is time to enter a new season, but something else comes first: hell in the hallway.

It has now been over twenty years since bright-eyed, twenty-one-year-old me started pastoring the church I still lead. In those two decades, I have been through enormous transition. Change, whether personal, corporate, or cultural, is difficult for any of us to navigate. Sometimes the magnitude of the change is so great that we surrender to the idea that such a transition is impossible. We may recognize that change demands things from us that we are not willing to do. Or, we may be discouraged by how often we have seen others fail when they attempted the transitions into which we are being led. Sometimes we have already committed to some change and think that further transition will just be too much to handle. Whatever change you are facing, excuses will never be in short supply. Yet if you push through these changes, you will find your breakthrough.

CHANGES IN THE CHURCH

The Book of Acts contains several moments of great transition in the early church. In Acts chapter 13 we see a transition centered around Saul (who later became known as the apostle Paul) and Barnabas, his partner on his first missionary journey. Watching them navigate this shifting season provides timeless lessons that can serve as reminders for what lies ahead.

Changing demographics

The demographics of the early church were changing. This primarily Jewish church was adding many Gentile members, which presented challenges because of their different backgrounds and radically divergent worldviews. For the leaders of the early church, moving from the kosher, unadulterated ears of the Jews, complete with their understanding of Old Testament principles, to the polytheistic, heathen ears of the Gentiles presented quite a challenge. Not only were the people different in religious backgrounds, they came from different ethnicities and cultures, which made this transition even more difficult.

Today, many leaders struggle with the changing demographics of their congregations. Sometimes leadership is resistant to change, but more often, resistance comes from church members who have grown used to worship in a homogenous setting. Our current culture attempts to divide people based on race or socioeconomic status, and that does not help these transitions either. However, the only alternative to seeking diversity in our congregations is to worship in divided groups that are not a reflection of the kingdom of God.

Changing epicenters

Not only was God changing the makeup of the early church, He was also changing the epicenter of their religious system. For centuries, worship had been centered in Jerusalem, but now the gospel was spreading to other locations like Antioch. While Jerusalem had been the location of the outpouring of the Holy Spirit on Pentecost, it was never meant to be the sole location of God's presence in the New Testament world. God's intention was that the move that started in the Upper Room would spill into the streets and spread across the globe, eventually carrying the redeeming power of Christ to the uttermost parts of the earth (Acts 1:8).

The challenges of the move outward from Jerusalem were indicative of a problem that still exists in the church. People get settled in places and attached to locales. We get stuck in the rut of routine and find ourselves spending year after year doing the same things in the same places and getting diminishing results. The early church scattered only when they faced persecution. We do not know whether or not they would have ever branched out without hardship. But we do know that too many of our churches today never do.

In this hour, God is raising up churches that have a different paradigm of operation. These churches are going to have leaders who walk in a different understanding of growth and seek a success that is not measured solely in temporal metrics. No longer is the focus going to be on growing the next megachurch. Instead, we are going to see leaders who are raising up mega-people. Churches who build mega-leaders in the marketplace will see a revival in the marketplace as godly men and women walk out their Christian faith in the public square. This is another aspect of the changing epicenter.

Changing leaders

Third, the narrative shows that God is changing leaders. No longer do just the twelve apostles lead the church. New leaders such as Paul and Barnabas who did not accompany Jesus during His earthly ministry emerged on the scene. Paul encountered Christ on the road to Damascus after the resurrection. Paul, who was a Jewish leader, then became the leader of the gospel of grace to the Gentile church. This was preparation for an explosion of souls getting saved, for churches being established, and for lives being transformed.

LESSONS FROM ANTIOCH

Changing leaders, changing congregations, and changing centers of ministry are all substantial alterations. These changes will most certainly not be easy. Times of transition are typically accompanied by some of the biggest spiritual battles that you will ever encounter. Thankfully, the record of the New Testament church in Acts gives us insight into how these trying times can be successfully handled. Changes were taking place in the church at Antioch. Doors of divine opportunity were getting ready to fly open.

At the center of all these changes was a man named Saul (later changed to Paul), who traversed the terrain of transition on a personal level so the church at large could benefit from his courageous decision to keep pressing forward. Paul lived an *after this* experience in almost every chapter of his life. Like you and me, he probably never grasped exactly what his saying yes to God did for the rest of those who belonged to the kingdom.

Prayer and fasting

The first lesson that the experience of the church in Antioch teaches us is that those who want to transition into more need a solid foundation of consecration for all that lies ahead. Let me say clearly that you will need to be a person of prayer and fasting in order to execute the divine purposes of God in your life.

> As they worshipped the Lord and fasted, the Holy Spirit said, "Set apart for Me Barnabas and Saul for the work to which I have called them." Then after

> fasting and praying, they laid their hands on them and sent them off.
>
> —ACTS 13:2–3, MEV

In Acts, these changes were occurring in a church body that was given to fasting and prayer. Friends, if there is anything that has remained steady since the first century, it is the fact that Christians who see kingdom advancement must be people of prayer and fasting. Even in the twenty-first century, believers and churches must come to the realization that there are no shortcuts, no flashy ways to circumvent this requirement. The only way to be part of what heaven is releasing on the church is to be seeking the Lord beyond the mediocre level of convenient spiritual activity.

Every generation has a land that God has determined for them to possess, a place of promise that goes beyond the present. Remember, God is the God of more. With the expanding territory for kingdom work must come leaders who rise to the necessary level to step into that territory. However, the qualification to fulfill the role is to be proactive with God's move, not reactive to circumstances. This necessary strategic download only occurs when we are walking in heavenly places, seeking God, and crucifying the deeds of our flesh. In other words, it happens when we are people of fasting and prayer.

We are agents of transformation working for the advancement of the kingdom. The God we serve never needs to be informed about what is happening, He never needs to catch up, and He is never reacting to the latest strategy or scheme of the devil. God is always in the future as the

Alpha and the Omega. Our ignorance about implementing strategy and structure that produces fruit and brings life only exists because we do not seek the One who has the answer. If we will but pray and fast, He will tell us who, where, and how to proceed. We must be humble enough to understand that this revelation only happens in the context of prayer and fasting.

Before you imagine that I am painting a pie-in-the-sky scenario in which change will be implemented without a challenge, please allow me to share the reality of moving forward. We may think that because we have a strategy informed by fasting and prayer, carrying it out it will be easy. The Book of Acts reminds us that this is not the case. Even when the transitions are in God's will and timing, we will still meet resistance. In fact, the more you hear from God, the more the enemy will fight you. The fact that you are hearing from God is what makes you such a threat to Satan.

Hell is never threatened by a church acting in its own power, strength, and ideas. You may have the latest strategy and all the best programs, products, and plans. Family, let me be real with you. Hell is not threatened by your cute church growth strategy or the five secrets to marketing you just picked up at the bookstore. Hell is nervous about a church that has received instruction from the Holy Spirit. Hell is disturbed when men and women step into the pulpit from a place of prayer, and they are coming with a download from heaven and a heart to obey. When hell sees those kinds of people, it will do everything it can to hinder the plan and purpose of God from being brought to pass. I know you thought you were past the *this* and in the *after this*, but remember, your anointing attracts the enemy.

Sending, not keeping

The church at Antioch was remarkable for a plethora of reasons, but something in particular stands out to me. This church measured their effectiveness and health, not by how many people they *kept*, but by how many they *sent*. For them, success in ministry was not in having a large crowd show up for their weekly gatherings. No, it was sending teams of missionaries to carry the gospel to new places.

For too long, the measure of church wellness has been fiscal and physical. We have been infatuated with buildings, crowds, and the size of the budget. I cannot tell you how many times I have been in a room in which pastors were asking about one another's assignments, with the only important answer being the weekly attendance. Brothers and sisters, God is calling us to a different way of thinking.

Now you are ready to transition. You have heard from God and have communicated the vision to the people around you. They are getting on board. You are about to see incredible things. But before you see that incredible future, prepare for an incredible fight. This is hell in the hallway.

HELL IN THE HALLWAY

Hallways are never intended to be places where we reside, entertain, or feed. They only serve to connect two or more different places, rooms, or, in this case, seasons. When you are in the hallway, you are not where you have been, and you are not yet where you are going. The hallway is the place of transition.

You may be in one of life's hallways right now. Chances are, you are not a person who likes change. Few of us do. I do not volunteer for it, but I have come to accept that change is an unavoidable reality for people who want to experience the moving of God. Whatever *here* you are in, it is not a permanent assignment. It may last a month or a year, but God will call you to a new place.

As you move from one assignment, calling, or season to another, you will spend time in the hallway. Do not set up camp there. Do not attempt to make this place of transition a place of comfort. The hallway is intended to be a temporary passage, not a home.

The temporary nature of the hallway notwithstanding, anyone who has ever experienced kingdom transition will tell you that hell raises its head in the hallway. But that is OK because when God is calling you into a new season, nothing can stop the change from happening and from you being part of it.

Perhaps you are entering the hallway. Change is happening. You have made up your mind that you are open and available to reach new audiences and touch new hearts. You are not staying stuck being the same kind of leader you have always been. You will not stay stuck worshipping in Jerusalem when Antioch is calling. You are going to make those changes, embrace change and transition, and become the version of you that God wants you to become. You are ready to be downloaded and updated, not stuck in the place where you have always been. You are prepared to be in a fresh place in God.

Let me tell you what is coming. When you make your mind up to move from where you have been, when you decide that you will not be stuck there anymore but instead will move forward, you are likely to face a few challenges. Knowing this might not bless you right now, but it will later when you have decisions to make. Transition can be tough, and there will be hell in the hallway. Even so, I want to testify that it does not last forever! What God started in you He will finish.

People will leave.

First, you will have to deal with a painful reality of transition. When you make up your mind to change and become everything God is calling you to be, not everyone who started with you will stay with you. A man named John went with Paul and Barnabas on their first missionary journey as a helper (Acts 13:5). But eight verses later, we read, "And John departed from them and returned to Jerusalem" (Acts 13:13, MEV). This was a painful loss for Paul and Barnabas. Nobody likes to accept the departure of people from their ministry, especially ones they love. None of you wants to believe that people who started with you could turn their backs on you and leave. When you launch out for another level and people begin to leave, you may be tempted to believe that you have lost your mind, that somehow you made the wrong decision. That is a lie of the enemy.

Never let the people who leave cause you to second-guess the vision God gave you. This vision was not supposed to be accomplished by the people who left but by the people who stayed. Do not get me wrong; this knowledge does not make it easy. I have been through some painful seasons during which people I thought would be with me forever left. I have wept and cried. I have tossed and turned in my bed. I have asked myself what I did wrong. You are not alone in those feelings. The bottom line is that some people cannot stay, and some people cannot go, but God will use whom He will, when He will, to advance His cause.

People leave for many reasons, and some will even leave because of the transitions God is directing. Some theologians believe John left Paul and Barnabas because he knew that the audience for the message was changing, and he grew nervous about being associated with ministry to the Gentiles. Had they continued to minister in the comfortable boundaries of the Jewish audience, those scholars allege that John would have never left.

If that is the case, his staying on would have put Paul and Barnabas in a difficult position. Would they be hindered in ministry because of their desire not to have someone who started with them leave? Or, would they pursue the purpose God was leading them to fulfill?

You will face decisions like this. When you do, always choose God's purpose. If you are in the hallway of transition and you are experiencing the pain of people leaving you there, let them go. Bless them, walk in honor, and release them. Do not allow yourself to grow bitter and do not lose your focus. Hell in the hallway does not mean God is finished. Continue to trust Him, and He will continue to work.

The enemy will stir up trouble.

In Acts, not only did people leave, but the enemy worked to stir up trouble as well.

> The word of the Lord was being spread throughout all the region. But the Jews stirred up the devout and prominent women and the chief men of the city, raised up persecution against Paul and Barnabas, and expelled them from their region.
>
> —Acts 13:49–50

Can you imagine being sent on a missionary journey, and at an early stop the people decide to throw you out and stir all the people up against you? Have you ever witnessed the enemy stirring things up to stop you? I have. I have been fully anointed for my assignment, and as I stepped into the pulpit, the atmosphere began to tighten. You could cut the spiritual tension with a knife. I have walked into meetings in which everyone in the room except me knew I was the primary subject on the day's agenda. These moments are never pleasant, but they are typical for life in the hallway. The enemy will stir up anything and anyone who will get to you. I have seen him stir up gossip. I have witnessed him stir up brothers and sisters in Christ. Satan will look for anything connected to you so that he can get to you.

I do not have to write a list of the things the enemy stirs up, and you do not have to label them. It is just mess, junk, demonic pressure, deadlines, ridiculous expectations, chatter, and toxic opinions. It is the stuff that builds up step-by-step as you walk through hell in the hallway until it feels as if you are at the point of breaking.

So, what do you do when the enemy has stirred things up? How do you get through the hallway when you can hear chatter coming from everywhere around you? You do what the apostles did in Acts 13:51: "So they shook the dust off their feet as a warning to them and went to Iconium" (NIV). When the enemy stirred it up, Paul and Barnabas shook it off and moved on.

This is not just a catchy saying. They literally shook the dust from that city off their feet. Why shake it off? You do not want to carry the residue of one season into the next season God has for you. When you go to the next level, you want to be rid of the stuff the enemy stirred up. Get alone with God and shake the stuff off. Today is the day to determine you are finished being distracted. Shake off the frustrations, the burdens, the bad news, and the false reports of the enemy. Shake them off.

The enemy wants all the stuff that got stirred up to stick to you. His plan is for your difficulties to make you bitter. But God does not want you to carry the dust of your prior pain into your place of purpose. With God, the very things that were meant to be your destruction will become another paragraph in your testimony. God is not done with you yet!

Let me declare the promises of God to some folks who have been suffering through hell in the hallway. You are coming out of pain and into joy. The Bible declares that the redeemed of the Lord shall return with joy upon their head (Isa. 51:11). Do not give up in the middle of this transition. You will step into the territory God has sent you to possess. The next verse after Paul and Barnabas shake the dust off their feet is this: "And the disciples were filled with joy and with the Holy Spirit" (Acts 13:52, MEV).

There is an *after this*. You will not always be stuck here. The Holy Spirit is confirming in you that the stuff that was stirred up will never stop you from doing all that He called you to do. The hallway is not forever. Shake it off and move forward.

You will choose praise or pride.

There remains a third place you may experience while walking through the hallway of your transition. This one is not painful like the first two, but it still must be navigated with care. It is demonstrated in Acts 14 as Paul and Barnabas find themselves in Lystra. A man who is lame from his birth hears Paul preaching. Faith begins to grow in the man's heart, and he jumps to his feet, healed (Acts 14:8–10). After the crowd watches Paul be used by God to heal a lame man, they call Paul and Barnabas gods that were sent down from above (Acts 14:11–13). But Paul and Barnabas are horrified to hear such things and rebuke the crowds.

In times of transition, the pain you have experienced becomes productivity. This man went from lameness to wholeness. In your hallway seasons, you will move from the place of rejection and conflict to a place of kingdom fruitfulness. But do not let down your guard. Be careful in those seasons when you experience breakthroughs and your work yields fruit. Why? Because your productivity will either produce praise or pride. You will either praise

God for what He has done or you will grow prideful over what you feel like are your accomplishments. If you know God did it and you are humble in your heart, you will give God praise. But if you are not careful when reading the press about the productivity God is giving you, you will start thinking you healed the lame man.

I have discovered that the antidote for pride is a robust worship life. I get really concerned when preachers stop worshipping Jesus and yet allow others to praise them. You can stick your head up and act as if it were you if you want to, but I choose to have tear-filled eyes, lifted hands, a grateful heart, and a mouth full of praise. In every success, I choose to give Him the glory. In every victorious ministry endeavor, I decide to give Him the praise.

It is dangerous to believe that something inherent in you produces the change in the broken lives around you. Let me remind you that "Pride goes before the destruction, and a haughty spirit before a fall" (Prov. 16:18, NIV). The first two attacks of the enemy in the hallway were attacks of depression, heaviness, darkness, and pressure as things were stirred up. But the third attack is old-fashioned pride.

The enemy thinks, "If I cannot get them to quit when people are leaving them, and if I cannot make them throw in the towel when people are stirring up stuff, maybe I can bait them into pride."

Rather than thinking we are gifts to the kingdom of God, we ought to remain grateful that He has even allowed us to be a part of His kingdom. Pastor, no matter how much your church is growing, no matter how productive you are in this season, be a worshipper. Be humble enough to be a person who praises. Do not buy into your own hype. The glory belongs to God. Let Him have all of it.

Some will turn against you.

Some Jews from the towns where Paul and Barnabas had previously been stirred up the crowds to turn against the apostles. They stoned Paul and left him for dead (Acts 14:19–20). What a turn of events! People who had just called Paul a god were now trying to take his life. How in the world could people exist in these two extremes?

People are fickle. The same ones who praised you on the last level will try to kill you when they see you making it to the next one. You are going to encounter moments in which you will scratch your head and wonder what you did, why they turned on you. Let me help you. You did not do anything. This is just another attack of the enemy. Often people resent your progress. Do not take it personally. God is still moving. The stones they throw will not kill you. This is just hell in the hallway.

THE PROMISE OF *AFTER THIS*

The Bible says Paul was lying down after being stoned, and the disciples stood around him. Then Paul stood up and went into the next city and began to minister the gospel again. You are not finished yet. This hallway of transition has tried to take you out, but you are not done yet. If you could see what is at the end of this hallway, you would set your mind to say, "I am getting out of this mess!" Get up. Keep moving into the next assignment, and you will see the hand of God move in a powerful way.

Paul went back to his home base of Antioch and testified to the church there how God opened the door of faith to the Gentiles. He had to go through the hallway to get to the open door. The hell in the hallway was worth it when he saw the cities of that region of their first missionary journey turned upside down by the gospel of Jesus. Yes, he fought hell in his time of transition. But in the end, he testified about how God had opened the door.

When God opens a door of a new season to you, do not stop in the hallway.

This book contains a promise of *after this*, and right now you believe it is coming. But first comes the hallway, which is the last place the enemy has to stop you before you break through into the goodness of God. Perhaps that explains the intensity of what you have been dealing with in this time of transition. He is going to fight as hard as he can. Let me tell you this one final time: Satan will never stop fighting, but he will always lose.

Family, it is time for your *after this*. You are walking through open doors right now! This season we have lived through has opened doors for men and women ministering the gospel. Walk through them and embrace the changes. You are going to feel the heat of hell as you walk through the hallways, but do not stop.

On the other side, you will testify to the faithfulness of God.

Conclusion

WE HAVE COME to the end of our time together, but we are nowhere near the end of our journey. As we find ourselves bidding farewell, I pray that you are walking away a different person. It is my hope that these pages have not only inspired you but also equipped you with some actionable changes in thinking you can use to navigate the seasons ahead with newfound vision.

What you have gleaned from these pages is far more than the means to arrive at a desired destination. While vision, forward thinking, and hope for tomorrow are all part of our walk of faith, this journey is more about our development than our arrival at a destination. It is possible to arrive at our goals without growing as individuals. If this occurs, we have not really gone anywhere, and whatever success we do encounter will be fleeting.

You may wonder why I would believe that personal

development is paramount to achieving life goals and fulfilling vision, especially since those things are a large part of the conversation in Christian circles. If you do not develop as an individual, you will not be equipped to handle substantial success and you will find yourself ill-prepared for kingdom service at the levels you need. With the right programs, persistence, and help from a good team, you can reach incredible heights, but what good is that if you have not developed the character necessary to dwell there?

This book has been about reaching the time of *after this*. Breakthrough moments will be inherited only by those of us who are faithful through the brokenness of whatever *this* is that precedes our triumph. What begins as a tumultuous journey filled with threats, fears, and frustrations becomes a walk of peace. What starts as the exposure of weakness and lack matures into seasons of strength and times of increase. The *after this* understanding reveals that life is found in places of sure death, struggle eventually gives way to overcoming, and victory is snatched from the jaws of sure defeat.

I have endeavored to leave you with helpful examples and practical illustrations from my experiences as well as Scripture. In all the biblical examples in this book, you will not find one in which the people of faith ended their race in defeat. In fact, I cannot recall any time that believers have ever been defeated, only times where they gave up before seeing the victory.

God has repeatedly shown that He is faithful to walk with His children through the difficult seasons and to bless them with new seasons when His timing and their character were aligned. As we look at the champions of the faith who went before us, we find common attributes in those who were ultimately victorious on their journey.

I do not want to leave you with the impression that I am recommending some mechanical list of action items, the fulfillment of which guarantees you success, however you may define it. Nonetheless, certain priorities must be maintained by those of us in pursuit of all God has for us. For those who have stepped into an *after this* season, we see the following truths in each of their lives.

THEY TRUST THE SCATTERING

The pioneers of the faith did not have a cake walk. They faced unthinkable persecution and nearly universal opposition. Despite these hardships, they did not entertain the thought that God had abandoned them. They never lost confidence that God was working His purpose in their lives. Even when they did not understand His works, they trusted Him.

The mothers and fathers who blazed kingdom paths believed that no matter what hand life dealt them, the sovereign hand of God was at work, scattering the gospel seed so the kingdom of God could grow. They understood that they brought the good seed in Christ's parable (Matt. 13:8). So being scattered was simply the carrying out of their divine purpose.

Remember, you are a seed—a potent, life-giving, kingdom-carrying seed that is intended to spring up and bear fruit that brings glory to the Master of the field. You are the good seed. Wherever life may lead you and whatever challenging ground you may find yourself cast upon, you are potent and you are there on purpose. You may not be able to see it, but God is at work through you. Trust that your heavenly Father knows how to maximize every ounce of possibility that lies within you. At times you will not recognize your own potential, but God does because He put it in you.

Of course, in the gaps between God's activation of your potential and your understanding of what He is doing, you may find yourself in circumstances that confound your reasoning. I imagine that some in the early church were confused about the scattering that occurred in their lives. But like them, we should decide to be fruitful and produce a harvest, no matter where we may be scattered.

THEY KEEP THEIR VISION

Imagine being Joshua and Caleb, listening to the Lord speak through Moses about the land of unimaginable abundance in your future. Imagine being one of the only ones to buy into what God was saying. Now, think about what it must have been like to be forced, by no fault of your own, to spend forty years wandering in the wilderness of frustration and unrealized potential. After four decades of waiting for prophetic words to come to pass, when they come to the very moment of promise, what is the first thing God says to Joshua and Caleb?

"The Lord said to Joshua, 'See, I have given Jericho, its king, and mighty men of valor into your hand'" (Josh. 6:2, MEV).

After forty years of mind-numbing life in the wilderness,

God raises one point of inquiry. Had the forty-year-old promise vanished in their hearts? Or could they still see with their spiritual eyes the promise He had made to them? Has their time with the doubters stolen their dedication? Have the naysayers caused them to think that maybe this was beyond their ability? Have the years surrounded by matriarchs of mediocrity and the fathers of fickle faith warped their perspective? Did they still have the vision?

Keep your vision, family! People who step into seasons of strength and blessing have maintained their vision. You must keep your spiritual eyes clear and focused. Fight every feeling that would cause your eyes to be downcast. Reject every voice that would distract you from what God is showing you. Resist every enemy who comes to steal your vision. You must be able to *see*!

You will encounter times of waiting, which are never enjoyable, but delays do not change the reality of God's promises, only our confidence in them. Hindrances will come, and sometimes from the most surprising of places. Your path will be full of flashy signs and roadside attractions that try to draw your eyes away from that which God has placed before you. Do not let any of these things shake you from knowing that, if God said it belongs to you, then it is yours.

THEY MAINTAIN A REVELATION OF THE GREATNESS OF GOD

I am well aware that many Christian books are filled with tired rhetoric and played-out platitudes, but this truth goes beyond that. It is vital that we preserve our understanding of the greatness of God, because within this revelation the key to Christian victory is found.

When we peruse the archives of Christian history, we find that those who lived glorious lives for God were never distracted by the size of their enemies. They never obsessed over the obstacles that lay in their paths. Rather, they were captivated by the awesome greatness of their God.

It is easy to lose our awareness of God's greatness as we navigate the trials and vicissitudes of this life. We must stay alert to this danger and constantly be working to see that we do not fall prey to it. If you discover that you are becoming selfish, myopic, or depending upon earthly strength, you must act to prevent losing the revelation of His greatness. Feed your heart a steady diet of His goodness. Train your mind to think first of His power and goodness, not all the reasons why you are doomed for failure. Feast on truths that will keep your spirit in a state of awe, and never fail to prioritize worship.

The psalmist reminds us that "Great is the LORD, and greatly to be praised" (Ps. 145:3, MEV). A robust revelation of the greatness of God will sustain you in the darkest of times.

THEY ADVANCE IN ADVERSITY

Hardship is coming. It may already be here. You may be reading this book while you are attempting to make your way through the most arduous paths you have ever traveled. You may feel as if you are surrounded on every side and just hanging on by a thread. It is likely that you have even thought that this current difficulty is a sure sign that either God did not really call you into new places, or at least that this is not the right timing.

Do not let difficulty dictate your divine task or its timing. What and when are for God to decide; they are not the prerogative of the enemy who is assailing you.

Whatever you do, do not wait until the struggle subsides before you decide to advance the purposes of God in the earth. If you are constantly hunkered down, waiting for the storm to pass before acting, you will never accomplish anything.

Adversity does not vanish simply because we are tired of it. Adversity begins to evaporate when the enemy discovers a tenacious perseverance in us. The church must stop waiting for the world to come into social, political, and generational alignment before we do our job. The spirit of this age will do all it can to prevent the formation of an environment that is conducive to the advancing of the Lamb's agenda. If it never gets easy, decide that you will never quit and that you will persevere in the things of God.

Sometimes you may be frustrated by the timing of God. Spiritual maturity is not revealed when we get what we want when we want it. True spiritual growth is evidenced when we honor God's purposes rather than focusing on what has not happened for us yet.

The author of your faith is the finisher of your faith. Do not quit on Him while He is writing the next chapter of your story. Glory, victory, breakthrough, and blessing are on the way—*after this*.

Notes

FOREWORD

1. Blue Letter Bible, s.v. "*patmos*," accessed August 20, 2021, https://www.blueletterbible.org/lexicon/g3963/kjv/tr/0-1.

CHAPTER 1

1. C. S. Lewis, *Mere Christianity* (New York: Macmillan Publishing Co., 1952), 31.
2. Blue Letter Bible, s.v. "*diōgmos*," accessed June 16, 2021, https://www.blueletterbible.org/lexicon/g1375/kjv/tr/0-1/; Blue Letter Bible, s.v. "*diōkō*," accessed June 16, 2021, https://www.blueletterbible.org/lexicon/g1377/kjv/tr/0-1/; Bill Wenstrom, "*Dioko*," Wenstrom Bible Ministries, accessed June 28, 2021, https://www.wenstrom.org/downloads/written/word_studies/greek/dioko.pdf.
3. John B. Polhill, *The New American Commentary: An Exegetical and Theological Exposition of Holy Scripture: Acts, vol. 26* (Nashville, TN: Broadman & Holman, 1992), 234.
4. James Montgomery Boice, *Acts: An Expositional Commentary* (Grand Rapids, MI: Baker Books, 1997), 132.
5. David Guzik, "Philip and the Samaritans," Blue Letter Bible, accessed June 29, 2021, https://www.blueletterbible.org/Comm/guzik_david/StudyGuide2017-Act/Act-8.cfm?a=1026001.

CHAPTER 2

1. Kristina Fiore, "Hazy on Ground-Glass Opacities? Here's What They Are," MedPage Today, May 29, 2020, https://www.medpagetoday.com/pulmonology/generalpulmonary/86751.

CHAPTER 3

1. Rabbi Simcha Prombaum, "Hineni: 'Here I Am' and 'I Am Here' Are Different," *Wisconsin Jewish Chronicle*, November 30, 2014, http://www.jewishchronicle.org/2014/11/30/hineni-here-i-am-and-i-am-here-are-different/.

CHAPTER 4

1. Blue Letter Bible, s.v. "*chalepos*," accessed June 29, 2021, https://www.blueletterbible.org/lexicon/g5467/kjv/tr/0-1/.

CHAPTER 5

1. Blue Letter Bible, s.v. "*Pereṣ*," accessed June 9, 2021, https://www.blueletterbible.org/lexicon/h6557/kjv/wlc/0-1.

CHAPTER 7

1. Blue Letter Bible, s.v. "*oikodomeō*," accessed June 29, 2021, https://www.blueletterbible.org/lexicon/g3618/kjv/tr/0-1/.
2. David Guzik, "Psalm 84—The Pilgrim's Love and Longing for God and His House," Enduring Word Bible Commentary, accessed June 29, 2021, https://enduringword.com/bible-commentary/psalm-84/.
3. Jacob Zallel Lauterbach, "Obed-Edom," *Jewish Encyclopedia*, accessed June 9, 2021, https://www.jewishencyclopedia.com/articles/11648-obed-edom.
4. Blue Letter Bible, s.v. "ʿāḵôr," accessed June 16, 2021, https://www.blueletterbible.org/lexicon/h5911/kjv/wlc/0-1/.
5. Blue Letter Bible, s.v. "*bᵊrāḵâ*," accessed June 16, 2021, https://www.blueletterbible.org/lexicon/h1293/kjv/wlc/0-1/.
6. Blue Letter Bible, s.v. "ʿōz," accessed June 16, 2021, https://www.blueletterbible.org/lexicon/h5797/kjv/wlc/0-1/.
7. Blue Letter Bible, s.v. "*hayil*," accessed June 16, 2021, https://www.blueletterbible.org/lexicon/h2428/kjv/wlc/0-1/.

KEVIN WALLACE

MINISTRIES

Bishop Kevin Wallace is the founder and pastor of Redemption to the Nations Church, a Christocentric, Spirit-empowered family of believers comprising many nations and generations.

In addition to serving the needs of thousands of parishioners domestically and globally each week, Bishop Wallace is the founder of the Ruach Global Network, an interactive virtual community of ministry leaders. He is a modern-day apostolic leader whose mission is fueled by the power of the Holy Spirit and whose motive is to see every leader function in his or her calling and anointing. Through the Ruach Global Network, Bishop Wallace and the Redemption to the Nations Church family host various conferences annually at which believers and leaders gather for powerful times of encounter and equipping.

A unique and powerful communication style has marked his ministry since he began preaching at seventeen years of age. After a successful evangelism ministry, he accepted his first pastoral assignment in 2003. His vision to be the most loving church in the world continues to be a catalyst for overcoming racial and generational barriers in our day. His messages of hope and healing are reaching locally and globally through an expanding digital ministry influence that includes television ministry, social media platforms, livestreams, and podcasts.

In his debut book, Kevin has filled these pages with life and truth: a new season will indeed commence "after this."

In spite of the vast demands on Bishop's life, his greatest joy in life is serving as a devoted husband to Deven and as a faithful father to their five children: Jeremiah, Isaiah, Zion, Judah, and Genesis. The Wallace family resides in Ooltewah, Tennessee.

For more information, visit:

www.KevinWallace.Live | www.RTTN.Church | www.RuachConference.com

@BishopKevinWallace | @RTTNPastor